HEGEL IN FRANCE

Michael Kelly,
Professor of French,
University of Southampton

BIRMINGHAM MODERN LANGUAGES PUBLICATIONS

©Michael Kelly
1992

First published 1992 by
Birmingham Modern Languages Publications
School of Modern Languages
University of Birmingham
Edgbaston
Birmingham B15 2TT
United Kingdom

ISBN 0 7044 1197 0

For Jo, Thomas and Paul

CONTENTS

INTRODUCTION

A short monograph in English on Hegel in France is a surprising and paradoxical undertaking. Surprising in that it has not already been done, comprehensively and in French; paradoxical in that it should be either short or in English. Perhaps there are too many reasons why it should have been done before now. The enormous importance of Hegelian thought in post-war France is unquestioned, even by those who have deplored it. Moreover, Hegel was virtually the inventor of the history of philosophy, and it may appear surprising that his French successors have not chosen to trace the course of his impact in their intellectual history. On the other hand, it may be a sign of the vitality of Hegelian ideas that French philosophers have been more concerned with putting them to work than with enquiring into their life history.

Certainly there are several partial studies in French, and a comprehensive study would be a dauntingly vast proposition for any scholar, touching as it does on virtually the entire history of French and European philosophy over almost two centuries. Moreover, it is by no means clear that a study of Hegel in France would be amenable to the methods of Hegelian history of philosophy. It is often supposed that Hegel considered his philosophy to be the culmination of the history of world philosophy, and therefore not admitting of a continuation. While this is an over-simple view, it is certainly difficult in a Hegelian perspective to embark on a sectoral study in the history of ideas without proposing to locate it within a general philosophical synthesis. Few contemporary philosophers would accept such an enterprise as either feasible or even legitimate. Perhaps the closest approximations have been the attempts to locate the history of ideas into a general *historical* synthesis, though in recent years the attraction of overarching global accounts of historical processes has noticeably waned. Nevertheless, a study in the history of ideas must acknowledge some conception of its own activity, especially when that activity is put in question by its object of study.

The conception adopted in the present study is that while ideas do have individual and collective histories, their history is not wholly their own. Hence, concepts, propositions, or arguments appear, change, and disappear at times and in places that can be charted, but their

1

development cannot be adequately understood in isolation from other historical processes, which provide both the conditions of intelligibility and the main motive force for change. Ideas, in other words, draw their life and strength more from social than from logical relations. How a particular set of ideas comes to be aggregated under the name of an individual thinker, such as Hegel, or of a movement, such as Hegelianism, is only partially to be explained by conceptual connections. What is more, the meaning and development of ideas identified as Hegelian cannot be grasped in abstraction from the history of the countries in which they have been discussed. And in the present case, it is their life in France which is at issue.

If ideas do not have their own history, it is difficult to deny that countries do. It may even provocatively be argued that having a history is what makes a country a country. The identity of a modern nation is closely bound up with the construction, by itself and others, of a historical narrative in which it figures as the subject. Philosophy is one of the cultural forms through which a nation represents itself, articulating a general statement of its own identity and its history, especially in relation to the acquisition of state power. In this sense, France has more philosophy, and therefore perhaps more history than most countries. However, a historical identity is primarily asserted in conflicts, or at least in differences. A nation identifies itself by distinguishing itself from its neighbours, and most especially from its enemies. France has substantially defined itself in the nature of its relations with its most immediate neighbours, and most visibly with the two most powerful of them, Britain and Germany, which have both at different times served as closest ally and deadliest enemy. It has often been remarked that France has experienced alternating enthusiasms for British and German philosophy, and there is indeed a clearly discernable relationship between French perceptions of Hegelian philosophy and France's relations with its German neighbours.

National identity is not separable, however, from a number of other identities which intersect it and qualify it. Though they are many and complex, it is possible to single out two major competing sources of identity: religious affiliation, usually rooted in family and community loyalties; and political commitment, usually based on the solidarities of social class. In both cases, the associated beliefs and values are articulated in sophisticated intellectual systems, frequently maintained at an international level, and capable of competing in force and complexity with dominant national philosophies.

The level of generality at which it is conducted makes philosophical activity highly transferable, with a wide, but not unlimited scope, for international exchange. It is one of the most fascinating aspects of Hegelian philosophy that it intervenes powerfully, though often ambiguously, in both the religious and the political discourse of France, offering a rich soil for several of the possible identities contending for dominance in France. In concrete terms, this has most often been argued out in terms of the relationship of Hegelian philosophy to Roman Catholic theology on the one hand and to socialist or communist political theory on the other hand.

Related to these issues, though not reducible to them, is the role of philosophy in forming a collective identity for the writers and artists who articulate the ideas and images with which the rest of society thinks and feels. These intellectuals specialise in the production and transmission of representations, and therefore have a strong interest in the metalanguages of writing about writing and writing about thinking. Hegel's intricate and imbricated conceptualisations have exercised a special attraction for French intellectuals, particularly in the areas of aesthetics and the history of philosophy. Both are disciplines which, if he did not invent them, Hegel at least endowed with a degree of authority which could not fail to appeal to the professionals of culture, who began to emerge during the nineteenth century as a distinct social stratum.

The detailed interrelation between this matrix of factors would require considerably more space to analyse than is available in this study, which must therefore stand as an outline sketch in the suggestive rather than the demonstrative mode. The picture which will unfold is of a slow, patchy and almost subterranean introduction of Hegelian ideas into France, against the grain of the dominant religious and political forces. As religious opposition declined in the second half of the nineteenth century, its place was taken by nationalist objections, linking with the suspicion of social subversion which attached to Hegel's reputation. The European Hegelian revival of the 1890s therefore found only a muted echo in France, and was mainly confined to the burgeoning socialist movement. It was not until the 1930s that a general upsurge of interest became noticeable, stemming from the phenomenological revitalisation of religious thought and from the renewal of socialist theory. Hegel became a major figure in postwar existentialist, Marxist and Catholic thought, and academic studies proliferated to swell the growing flood of work on him from many perspectives which continued throughout the 1960s and 1970s. At the same time there were influential philosophical attacks on Hegelian ideas, and the 1980s in particular witnessed a number of assaults on Master Narratives, of which Hegel's is perhaps the most comprehensive. But if anything this attention served to reinvigorate the study of Hegel, at least within the University, and his work continues to provide a major point of reference on both political and religious matters.

Whether the German philosophy professor who died in 1831 would have recognised himself in positions advanced in recent French debates is a nice but unanswerable question. And ultimately meaningless, since the 'Hegel' who became one of the 'three H's' of French philosophy (with Husserl and Heidegger) was primarily a body of texts, mostly in French, and a group of intellectual traditions in constant development. Real and often passionate differences subsist between the different strands of thought which have taken Hegel seriously, particularly between philosophers in the Marxist, Catholic and phenomenological traditions. However, in recent years these strands have largely ceased to be separate and self-sustaining intellectual communities. Political and ideological shifts on the larger stage have played a part in this, though in many respects the driving force has been the growing professionalisation of intellectual life which has brought divergent traditions together within common institutional structures. Nor has this process been confined to France, as the philosophers of continental Europe have increasingly developed cross-border links, and the French debates can now less readily be separated from those in Belgium, Switzerland, Germany or Italy, or from debates on a wider international scale.

The history of Hegel in France demonstrates the ability of Hegelian ideas to offer a common language to intellectuals from a wide range of ideological and national affiliations. It may be adventurous to speak of a philosophical or intellectual process of European integration, but the French experience suggests that Hegel has already become very much part of just such a process.

Michael Kelly
University of Southampton

CHAPTER ONE
HEGEL IN FRENCH

The development of Hegelian ideas in French thought has always been conditioned by the forms of relation between French and German culture. And while it is necessary to trace the written and published record, it is well to remember that this is only a partial index of the whole picture, and must be completed by the other forms of cultural exchange, especially the oral forms, for the early decades, and the audiovisual forms, for the most recent period.

In the early nineteenth century the primary forms of intercultural relation were based on personal contact, and only indirect and inconvenient records of this activity are available. The circulation of ideas depended on social gatherings, individual travel and orally delivered lectures, before assuming written form in letters, reports, lecture notes, reviews, articles and books. In the early part of the nineteenth century, Hegel's reputation in France depended on a small number of scholars travelling between the two countries. These included Hegel himself and the dominant force in French philosophy, Victor Cousin, but also a number of lesser figures of various nationalities: French and German philosophers, French germanists, German francophiles, Swiss and Italian philosophers, and émigrés from various European countries. In consequence, French perceptions of Hegel were refracted though a range of intermediaries who sought to enlist him in their own diverse causes.

The opacity of the screen of intermediaries was intensified by the fundamental problem of language. Whereas most educated Europeans could be expected to speak French, few educated French people, outside the Eastern provinces of Alsace and Lorraine, spoke German. Most French writers were therefore dependent on secondary sources or on translations, often provided by non-French speakers. It need hardly be added that the notorious complexity of Hegel's writing compounded the difficulty. Contact with Hegel's thought was therefore largely a second-hand affair. The view of Hegel presented by his various commentators will be examined in subsequent chapters, but it will be useful now to review the availability of translations of his work into French.

While some copies of the original German editions were obtainable by specialists in France, little of Hegel's writing was translated before the Second Empire, and most of what then became available was in translations of dubious fidelity. Charles-Magloire Bénard's rendering of the lectures on Art, *Cours d'esthétique*, was the first work by Hegel to appear in French,[1] some ten years after Hegel's death. Published in three volumes in 1840, 1848 and 1851, it was not so much a translation as a curious combination of summary, translation, paraphrase and commentary. Bénard was an eclectic and made clear that he considered Hegel's indiviual analyses to be separable from his overall system. In a similar spirit he rejected what he took to be the equation of history with logic in Hegel's philosophy. Bénard went on to prepare a scholarly translation of the material, which like all subsequent nineteenth century translations of Hegel was published by Ladrange and their successors Baillière. The weighty two-volume edition of *Esthétique* (1855) was also used as the basis for editions of extracted material, *La Poétique* (1855) and *Système des beaux arts* (1860). A second edition was published in 1875. It is perhaps curious that the most readily available works in French have been Hegel's lectures on Art, which, as well as being the first, are also the most translated and the most extracted. It is also likely that they are the most widely distributed and read. In part it is no doubt to be explained by the philosophical armature, which is perhaps less intimidating here than in other works. The lectures are therefore more accessible in form, as well as more appealing in content to readers whose interests are literary and artistic rather than strictly philosophical. In part too, it is connected with the fact that literary discussions were usually less rigidly policed, and ideas could be discussed there which would be inadmissible in philosophical circles.

The early 1850s also saw the publication of a short section on Logic from Hegel's shorter *Encyclopedia*, *La Logique subjective de Hégel*. Apart from the curiosity of the acute accent on the author's name, which lingered intermittently throughout the century, the translation is remarkable in being partly the work of an English scholar, H. Sloman, who also appended substantial explanatory remarks.

The main work of translating Hegel into French was undertaken by an Italian, the Tuscan philosopher Augusto Véra. Over a period of twenty years from 1859 to 1878, he published in French the three parts of Hegel's longer *Encyclopedia*, as well as his *Lectures on the Philosophy of Religion*. Each volume was accompanied by an apparatus of extensive commentaries and a lengthy explanatory introduction. The nine bulky tomes remained the major primary source for the study of Hegel's philosophy in France until the Second World War. Important though they

---

[1] Fuller details of translations are given in the appendix.

were historically, it is clear that Véra's translations did less than justice to his master. His qualifications for undertaking them were not negligible, since he held a French doctorat-ès-lettres and taught philosophy in France for some fourteen years before returning to his native Italy in 1860. But the mammoth labour of erudition fell considerably short of the standards which might be expected a century later. Alexandre Koyré's rather waspish description of Véra as 'un disciple plus enthousiaste que compétent' was doubtless justified by the notorious prevalence of misunderstandings and mistranslations.[2] But as he spoke, in 1931, Koyre could not point to any replacement, or indeed any other major translation of Hegel into French since Véra's. It was therefore with these imperfect instruments that Hegel's destiny in France was shaped.

Remarkably, Véra's final volume was the last French translation of Hegel to appear for fifty years. The silence was broken only in 1928, when the Romanian philosopher Dimitriu Rosca published a minor text, *La Vie de Jésus*, as a pendant to his French doctoral thesis. Paul Archambault's early popularisation of Hegel (1912) was obliged to draw largely on Véra's translation for its selection of texts. However, by the time the centenary celebrations of 1931 were over, substantial enterprises were being envisaged. A brief extract from the *Phenomenology of Mind* had already appeared in Jean Wahl's influential work on the unhappy consciousness (1929), a harbinger of greater things to come. Jean Gibelin published the first of his translations of Hegel's lectures, *The Philosophy of History*, with Vrin in 1937, and two young Marxist intellectuals, Henri Lefebvre and Norbert Guterman, produced a series of new translations of important passages in their *Morceaux choisis* of 1939 for Gallimard.

The three texts usually regarded as Hegel's major works, *Phenomenology of Mind*, *Philosophy of Right*, and *Science of Logic* finally all appeared over a period of ten years, to provide textual material for the Hegel revival which was such a prominent feature of the postwar intellectual scene. When Jean Hyppolite's translation of *La phénoménologie de l'esprit* appeared in two volumes with Aubier-Montaigne, in 1939 and 1941, it set new standards for philosophical translation, embodying as it did a wealth of careful exegesis. Its publication was hailed as an important philosophical event, though the circumstances of wartime France rather delayed its impact, and it has remained not only the authoritative translation of the *Phenomenology*, but also a yardstick by which other translations are judged. Andre Kaan's translation of the *Principes de la philosophie du droit* was published by Gallimard at the same inauspicious moment but quickly became the working document for the study of Hegel's political theory. Finally in

2 See Koyré, 'Rapport sur l'état des études hégéliennes en France', 1931. Fuller bibliographical details are contained in the appropriate appendix.

1947 and 1949, Aubier published Serge Jankélévitch's translation in two volumes of the *Science de la logique*, making available Hegel's major exposition of his philosophical system and its logic.

By the end of the 1950s, Jean Gibelin completed the energetic work of translation begun in the 1930s, which comprised the shorter *Encyclopedia* (Vrin, 1952) and almost all of the lectures, adding those on *Aesthetics* (Aubier, 1944), the *History of Philosophy* (Gallimard, 1954), and the *Philosophy of Religion* (Vrin, 1954-9) to his earlier rendering of the lectures on the *Philosophy of History* (Vrin, 1937). The *Esthétique* of 1944 was notable for being the first Hegel text to appear in a new translation, the centenarian Bénard version no longer meeting modern needs. However, dissatisfactions soon emerged with Gibelin's own rendering, and Jankélévitch, who had translated the last quarter of the *Esthétique*, was subsequently charged with producing a third translation of the work, which began appearing in 1964, and replaced the earlier version on Aubier's lists. The early post-war period also saw the translation of a number of minor works, especially those written early in Hegel's career and reflecting his religious preoccupations. These included *Les Preuves de l'existence de Dieu* (Aubier, 1947), *L'Esprit du christianisme et son destin* (Vrin, 1948), and *Premières publications* (Vrin, 1952).

With the publication in 1963 by the Editions de Minuit of the *Propédeutique philosophique*, translated by Maurice de Gandillac, and the appearance between 1962 and 1967 of the three volume *Correspondance*, for Gallimard, Hegel's main writings were all readily available in French. Already the process of refining the corpus had begun, and was to continue with a steady stream of translations of lesser known and minor works, including the first version of his major *Logic*, and important works from his early career at Jena (1801-07).[3]   At the same time retranslations appeared of major works. The *Esthétique* has already been mentioned, and Gibelin's other publications were gradually superseded: the lectures on the philosophy of history (translated by Papaioannou for 10/18, 1965), those on the history of philosophy (by Garniron for Vrin, 1971-78), and the shorter *Encyclopedia* (by Gandillac for Gallimard, 1970). The Gibelin versions of all but the lectures on art continue, however, to be reprinted by their respective publishers. Vrin finally replaced Véra's rendering of the 'shorter' *Logic* from the *Encyclopedia* by Bernard Bourgeois's translation in 1970, just after the entire set of Véra's original translations had been reprinted in facsimile. They eventually published a new *Philosophy of Mind* from the *Encyclopedia* in 1988, having meanwhile produced their own translation of the *Philosophy of Right,* which appeared in 1975.

---

[3] These are listed in the appendix.

The number of bulky scholarly editions from Vrin, Gallimard and Aubier has continued to grow with no perceptible slackening throughout the 1970s and 1980s, though as yet no attempt has been made to embark on an edition of the collective works. In the meantime, Hegel's writings were also beginning to appear in more accessible form in general or thematic collections, such as students might be expected to purchase. The Presses Universitaires de France were not surprisingly active in this domain from an early date, with *Hegel, sa vie, son oeuvre* (1949 and 1967), followed by collections on aesthetics (1954), philosophy of history (1975) and ethics and politics (1977). Other publishers followed their example, with selections appearing on aesthetics (1964) and politics (1975, 1977). In response to pressure from school and university requirements, Aubier began to publish a small number of texts in bilingual editions, with the French and German texts presented on facing pages so that readers with some knowledge of German could plot the conceptual complexities with more precision. This treatment has been given to sections from the *Phenomenology* (1966, 1977, 1989), the *Philosophy of Right* (1989) and lectures on Plato (1976).

The mid-1960s also saw the first appearance of Hegel in cheap paperback editions, notably in Gallimard's 'Idees' collection, which published four texts, but also Denoël-Gonthier's 'Médiations', Flammarion's 'Champ philosophique', and UGE's '10/18'. Selections from Hegel are now even available in the popular Livre de Poche collection. These publications are significant in that they have made Hegel accessible to a mass readership, and are an important channel through which Hegelian ideas have entered general circulation in France. They also provide an index of the substantial market which clearly exists for his ideas within and beyond the education system.

CHAPTER TWO
HEGEL AND FRANCE 1800-1848

Hegel was a child of the French Revolution. When it broke out, he was nineteen years of age and a student at the theological seminary of Tübingen. There he, and his later rival Schelling, were leading participants in the students' political club which discussed the debates of the French National Assembly, celebrated the anniversary of the storming of the Bastille and taunted émigré French aristocrats. One day Hegel and Schelling planted a 'tree of liberty'[1] in the town to honour the Revolution whose slogans were constantly on their lips. Some commentators have dismissed these activities as youthful enthusiasms soon cast aside, but Hegel's later writings confirm that the example of revolutionary France remained a constitutive element in his complex and ambivalent philosophy. In it, the idea of France revolved around this event which he considered to be a watershed in world history, with its roots in the philosophy of the Enlightenment and its fruits in the victorious advance of the armies of the Republic, and later of the Empire. Much of the puzzling ambiguity of Hegel's thought can be seen in his relentless attempt to encompass in a global synthesis both the subversive, critical rationality of the *philosophes* and the conservative, legitimising rationality of the authoritarian state.

Hegel saw himself as the legitimate heir of Montesquieu, Voltaire, Rousseau, D'Holbach and Diderot, whose works he read avidly as a student in Tübingen (1788-93) and whom he viewed as the fathers of the Revolution.[2] He read the works of many lesser figures in the Revolutionary movement, especially the Girondins,[3] as well as the debates of the Assemblée. And he welcomed the advance of France's revolutionary armies sweeping away so much of the decaying feudal structure of Europe. He saw Napoleon's triumphs as an expression of historical necessity, and even applauded the French victory at Jena where he was putting the finishing touches to his *Phenomenology*. However, his feelings were mixed, not only with dismay at the

[1] See Stern, Alfred, 'Hegel et les idées de 1789', 1939; and D'Hondt, *De Hegel à Marx*, 1972.
[2] For greater detail, see Lukács, *The Young Hegel*, 1975.
[3] See D'Hondt, *Hegel secret*, 1968.

discomfiture of his own native Germany, but also with abhorrence of the brutality which accompanied the forward march of history.

Hegel went on to develop philosophical positions which consciously built on the conceptual resources of the German language, and which specifically addressed problems of German social and cultural life. Nonetheless, his intellectual roots in French thought and French history provide a number of points of linkage between his work and the concerns of French philosophy. Paradoxically, however, they were links which inhibited as much as they promoted his acceptance by his French contemporaries. For much of the nineteenth century, official French philosophy implemented an undeclared embargo on the thought of the *philosophes*, whose free-thinking critiques of religious and political institutions were considered dangerous, leading to atheism and subversion. Dissenting intellectuals outside the University were less resistant to the political implications, though they frequently had religious qualms about Hegel's thought, and at times saw him as the apologist for an authoritarian state. Official enthusiasm for the Revolution had its moments, mainly in the latter part of the century, but French philosophers were generally prudent and broached such matters only with extreme care. Consequently, Hegel's French connections scarcely endeared him to French philosophers, even when they could overcome their nationalistic resistance to the philosophy of a country with which they were so often at odds, or even at war.

During his own lifetime, Hegel's impact on French philosophy began most auspiciously, thanks to his close relations with Victor Cousin, the leading figure in French academic philosophy of the Restoration period. Having virtually liquidated all traces of the enlightenment tradition, the newly established University institutions were casting about for a new intellectual framework. Cousin, the most dynamic of the new generation of philosophers, took on the task of knitting together the best elements in European thought. Having, as he felt, exhausted the resources of Scottish philosophy and Kant, he travelled to Germany in 1817 to investigate the new movements around Schelling, learning German for the purpose. When he met Hegel by chance in Heidelberg, Cousin was exhilarated and impressed by the philosopher, whom he declared a genius, and returned to Paris enthused by Hegelian ideas, at least as far as he had been able to understand them. He returned again the following year, and many of the ideas he found were immediately incorporated into his lectures. During the early 1820s, after Cousin's liberal views had led to his dismissal from the University, he made further visits. When in 1824 he fell foul of the Prussian police, who suspected him of spreading seditious *carbonarist* views, it was Hegel's intervention which eventually secured his release after six months of imprisonment. When Hegel visited Paris in 1827

Cousin was delighted to take charge of him. Cousin's lectures of 1828-9 after his reinstatement in the University were laden with Hegelian notions, which the eclectic approach easily accommodated. Intellectually, it was probably their shared commitment to the history of philosophy which formed the principal bond between the two thinkers, though they both occupied the uneasy position of intellectuals who combined a prominent public position with radical private views they shrank from spelling out clearly.

Aware that he was sailing close to the wind, Cousin took some care not to let his Hegelian inspiration obtrude too much, to the point where his unacknowledged borrowings drew accusations of plagiarism. With the advent of the July Monarchy Cousin was able to acknowledge his contact with Hegel and the resemblances in their work, though he insisted there were fundamental differences between them, and emphasised his own respect for Schelling.[4] He was, he claimed, unsure whether Hegel's relation to Schelling should be seen as Aristotle's to Plato or as Wolff's to Leibniz. Schelling, recalled from retirement to combat Hegelian influence in Berlin, was happy to write a preface for a German translation of Cousin's *Fragments philosophiques*, and expressed his satisfaction that Cousin had curbed his enthusiasm for Hegel.[5]

Elevated to an unrivalled academic and administrative preeminence over French education which he enjoyed for most of the next two decades, Cousin rapidly shed his more adventurous views. All explicit reference to Hegel was eradicated, and the relationship was only admitted as a personal anecdote. In a sense, therefore, Hegel was woven into the intellectual framework of academic philosophy from the beginning, although his presence was largely anonymous.

Cousin's patronage of Hegelian ideas was a powerful influence, but in many respects a mixed blessing. In the first instance it set the tone of an 'under the counter' arrangement, and tended to inhibit a direct encounter with Hegel's own works, which in any case were not available in French,[6] although Cousin could very well have commissioned translations. Secondly, Cousin's mediation imposed an eclectic framework on the encounter, which ran directly against the systematic and synthesising character of Hegel's work. And thirdly, Cousin's *imprimatur*, however cloaked, marked Hegel's reputation with the

---

[4] See Cousin, *Fragments philosophiques*, 2nd edition, 1833. Especially the new Preface, p.xxxvij-xlii.

[5] Schelling, 'Jugement de Schelling sur la philosophie de M. Cousin ...', 1835.

[6] See Chapter 2. The first translation of any kind appeared in 1840, but only the lectures on aesthetics were available before the Second Empire.

cultural authoritarianism and political conservatism of Cousin's own later career.

But Cousin's major achievement was not so much his own body of thought as the many works which he stimulated in others. It was probably he who encouraged the Italian Augusto Véra to pursue his highly fruitful study of Hegel. He certainly encouraged the Alsacian Joseph Willm, a schools inspector, a Lutheran, and director of the *Revue germanique*, who during the 1830s and 1840s wrote numerous articles and an important monograph on Hegel, as well as his four-volume history of German philosophy, which with Cousin's assistance gained a prize from the *Académie*. The Orleanist statesman Count Charles de Rémusat also enjoyed Cousin's support for his study of German philosophy (1845), which highlighted the scientific value of Hegel. Cousin received and encouraged the leading German Hegelians Edouard Gans, and Karl-Ludwig Michelet. And it was through Cousin's efforts that Hegel's thought became known to such writers as Jules Michelet, Edgar Quinet, Prosper Enfantin and Pierre-Joseph Proudhon,[7] and to the many others who studied philosophy in the 1820s, 1830s or 1840s.

Eugène Lerminier, then a liberal jurist with Saint-Simonian leanings, was one of the handful of French scholars to attend Hegel's lectures in Berlin. He was the first to give a clear presentation of Hegel's ideas in French, in 1831. He regretted what he saw as their conservatism, based on a retrospective rationalisation of events, which he thought had excercised a reactionary effect on Cousin.[8] Nonetheless, he recognised the power of the Hegelian synthesis, which no French contemporary could match, and the enthusiastic summary of Hegel's thought in his *Au-delà du Rhin* (1835) carried all the more authority because Lerminier was by then a professor at the Collège de France.

Two other Saint-Simonians, Jules Lechevalier and Gustave d'Eichtal, also attended some of the Berlin lectures, and pointed out to their colleagues the striking parallels which existed between Hegel and Saint-Simon. Auguste Comte was among those who learned of Hegel's thought in this way in the mid-1820s. He was attracted by it, and was gratified that Hegel had thought well of one of Comte's works. The contact was not pursued, however, since Comte was then breaking with the Saint-Simonians who were the principal intermediaries. Some commentators have suggested that Hegel's pantheistic notion of the

---

[7] See Eckles, 'La fortune intellectuelle de Hegel en France au dix-neuvième siècle', 1952.

[8] See Lerminier, *Philosophie du droit*, 1831; and *Lettres philosophiques adressées à un Berlinois*, 1832.

Incarnation of God in Man may have helped to spark the subsequent degeneration of the Saint-Simonians into religious mysticism, under the charismatic Enfantin.[9]

Hegel's thought also entered French social thought through émigré sources. There was a large influx of German-speaking political refugees in the early 1840s, many of them Young Hegelians like Friedrich Engels, Karl Marx and Arnold Ruge, but also activists like the young anarchist Mikhail Bakunin, who arrived from Russia via Switzerland, freshly imbued with a convert's enthusiam for Hegel. Though they did establish contact with French socialists, they had only a limited impact on French intellectual life. Most widely known in France was no doubt the German poet Heinrich Heine, who lived for many years in Paris and served as a self-appointed cultural ambassador between the two countries. He regarded Hegel as 'the greatest philosopher Germany has produced since Leibniz',[10] though Heine was more connected with literary than philosophical circles.

More influential intellectually was the Polish economist Count Auguste Cieszkowski. A disciple of Karl-Ludwig Michelet and a founder of the *Crédit foncier français*, Cieszkowski had written an imposing thesis in German proposing the transcendence of Hegel's philosophy of history in a philosophy of action.[11] In 1839 he published in French a treatise on credit and circulation, which deployed the Hegelian dialectic impressively in economic analysis. The book was widely influential and certainly had an impact on Proudhon, whose own work on economics began to graft Hegelian concepts on to its Kantian base. At the time of writing his *Qu'est-ce que la propriété?* (1840), Proudhon was already familiar with Hegelian ideas from reviews and reports, and his acquaintance improved through contact with Marx and, especially, Bakunin. His *Système des contradictions économiques, ou philosophie de la misère* (1846) was unmistakeably Hegelian in tone, even if, in his celebrated polemical response, *Misère de la philosophie* (1847), Karl Marx could reproach Proudhon for his poor grasp of the dialectic.

The leading French socialist philosopher of the period, Pierre Leroux, took a serious interest in Hegel's work, and recognised the importance of his philosophy of history, and of his idea of human perfectibility. However, Leroux was repelled by its schematic formulation, by its closeness to Cousin's eclecticism, which he roundly

---

9   See D'Hondt, *De Hegel à Marx*, 1972.
10   Heine, *De l'Allemagne*, 1835, vol. 1, p.224.
11   See Kolakowski, *Main Currents of Marxism*, vol. 1, 1978, pp.85-88.

attacked, and by its apparent pantheism.[12] Like many socialists of his generation, Leroux was a fervent believer in religion, albeit of a humanistic post-Christian variety. The rational and historical approach of Hegel (and Cousin) severed the link between religion and philosophy and could, he argued, only produce a pantheistic religion of nature, which was barely a shade removed from atheism.

Leroux was joined in his objections by more traditional Catholic commentators such as Lammenais, who had heard of Hegel as 'the Antichrist's Plato';[13] the *abbé* Maret, whose much reprinted *Essai sur le panthéisme* (1839) included a forthright denunciation of Hegel's pantheistic philosophy; and Amand Saintes, who along with Dr Gros, accused Hegel of a pernicious rationalism which applied the logic of the finite to the infinite and thereby undermined the notions of a personal God and an immortal soul, ultimately imperilling Christianity itself.[14] Louis Prévost, who had also attended some of Hegel's lectures, prefaced his thesis on Hegel's thought (1844) by protesting against its religious and moral consequences. Similar objections were loudly voiced when Emile Littré published his translation of Strauss's *Vie de Jésus* (1839-40). While Littré, a positivist and agnostic, was not a supporter of the very metaphysical Hegelianism of the book, he admired the rational and historical approach to religion which it contained. On the other hand, this epitomised all that spiritualist intellectuals, including the liberal Quinet,[15] found objectionable in Hegel. Auguste Ott, in a lengthy examination of Hegel's system (1844), was not the only commentator to lay the blame at the door of Protestantism.

Not all Catholics held religious objections to Hegel, however, and the Franco-German Young Hegelian Karl-Ludwig Michelet played an important role in defending Hegel's religious orthodoxy. A convert to Catholicism and a friend of Cousin, Michelet acquired considerable influence in France through his prize winning essay on the origins of the dialectic in Artistotle (1836). The Genevan Catholic Amédée Prévost defended Hegel against the charge of pantheism in Lechevalier's journal (1834). And the Breton Catholic Barchou de Penhoën mounted a staunch defence of Hegel's achievement in his important survey of German idealist philosophy (1836), though he could scarcely conceal his

---

[12] See Leroux, *Réfutation de l'eclectisme*, 1839, and 'Du cours de philosophie de Schelling', 1842.
[13] Lammenais, *Correspondance*, II, Paris, 1863, 125, quoted by D'Hondt, De Hegel à Marx, 1972.
[14] See Gros, *De la personnalité de Dieu et de l'immortalité de l'âme*, 1841; and Saintes, *Histoire critique du rationalisme en Allemagne depuis son origine jusqu'à nos jours*, 1841.
[15] See Quinet, 'De la vie de Jésus par le docteur Strauss', 1838.

own inclination towards a touch of pantheism in the mould of Schelling, which was a common tendency of the eclectic school.

As the 1840s progressed, Hegel's reputation came to be increasingly associated with the political situation in Germany. The influential liberal periodical, *La Revue des deux mondes*, kept a regular eye on philosophical developments across the Rhine, and in the ten years from 1843 published frequent assessments by Saint-René Taillandier.[16] Perceiving the importance of Schelling's recall to Berlin in order to combat Hegelianism, Taillandier linked the philosophy chair at Berlin to Prussian attempts to unify Germany under its own leadership. Hegel's tenure had, he thought, been decisive, and the divisions between Left and Right Hegelians were a reflection of the battle for political leadership within Prussia. The failure of Right Hegelians had prompted the Prussian aristocracy to fall back on Schelling and expel the leading Left Hegelians.

From this time, in France, Hegel's name became increasingly synonymous with both the growing power of Prussia and the rise of revolutionary movements in Germany. How this apparently contradictory reputation could emerge is suggested in a shrewd appraisal of Hegel's successors by A. Lèbre (1843), also in the *Revue des deux mondes*. He admired the austerity, depth and power of Hegel's thought, but pointed to the religious and political radicalism of the Left-wing Young Hegelians as a logical outcome, concluding with a comment which encapsulates much of Hegel's ambiguous legacy:

> All that is real is rational, all that is rational is real, he had said. Armed with this principle, one may strive to maintain the status quo and to justify progress of any kind, to remain stationary and to stir up revolutions, to legitimise political quietism as well as the impatient zeal for change.[17]

As a result, Hegel was twice damned. First, for his political conservatism, which was seen as indissociable from the advance of Prussian nationalism; second, for his political radicalism, which, though clearly German, was seen as all too transferable to revolutionary movements in other countries too. It is true that Hegelian echoes can be found in the French nationalism of Jules Michelet and the messianic Slav nationalism of Adam Mickiewicz, who both had their lectures at the Collège de France suspended, Mickiewicz in 1844, Michelet in January

---

[16] See Taillandier's articles of 1843, 1844 (three), 1847, 1848, 1850 (two), and 1853.

[17] Lèbre, 'Crise actuelle de la philosophie allemande: Ecole de Hegel, nouveau système de Schelling', 1843, p.18.

1848. But the predominant image of Hegelianism in France on the eve of 1848, the Year of Revolutions, was as a potent revolutionary idea, posing a threat to Church and State alike.

This association was neither wholly just nor wholly unfounded, but it sealed the fate of Hegel's reputation in France for more than a decade. It is well reflected in a short story entitled 'L'Hégélien' by Countess Valéry de Gasparin. Set in the spring of 1849, the story is narrated by a devout, conservative French gentlewoman, who describes her encounter with the dangerous but dashing captain of a revolutionary militia unit, while travelling through Switzerland to Germany. The Hegelian captain reveals his pantheistic and egalitarian ideals, and offers the travellers safe-conduct, which they decline, before he disappears over the Rhine to join his unit. The French woman is stirred to see the proud Prussian army mustering, but her emotions are mixed as she hears of the thoroughness with which the revolutionaries have been pursued and executed. Though published in 1858, the story vividly captures the *frisson* which the name of Hegel could cause for a decade after 1848.

CHAPTER THREE
HEGEL UNDER THE SECOND REPUBLIC AND
SECOND EMPIRE 1848-1870

The revolution of 1848 brought a rapid end to the July Monarchy and an equally rapid end, for the time being, to the rationalist spiritualism which had dominated the French education system for almost twenty years. For a brief moment the liberals and socialists enjoyed unprecedented opportunities to stamp their mark on French life and thought, before being driven back into silence or exile by the authoritarian régime of Louis-Napoléon, whose intellectual parameters were set by Catholic clericalism and Saint-Simonian technocracy.

For Hegel's following in France the rise and fall of the Second Republic brought disaster in several forms. The Republican upsurge swept from power Victor Cousin and the Orleanist eclecticism which had been more or less covertly spreading Hegelian ideas. The *loi Falloux* handed education over to revanchist clergy who were keen to root out unorthodoxy, especially in the form of pantheistic residues. The new élite of the Second Empire were often positivists who would brook no talk of metaphysics, and saw philosophy as useful only as a training in logic. The continued rise of Prussian dominance in Germany cast a shadow over the philosopher who was regarded as its main apologist. And at the same time Hegelianism was clearly identified as a doctrine with revolutionary implications at a time when the open avowal of socialism was an act of personal disqualification.

The advent of the Second Empire did not entirely eliminate the people or ideas that fell from grace, but it ensured them a difficult life, with less access to the public forums on which intellectual life depends. The case of Etienne Vacherot is a striking illustration. His magisterial history of the Alexandrian school of Greek philosophers was steeped in a dialectical metaphysics strikingly close to Hegel's own, but the publication of the third volume in 1851 sparked a storm of Catholic protest which produced Vacherot's dismissal from the Ecole Normale.

He continued to develop his doctrine of 'positive metaphysics',[1] but remained socially and intellectually marginalised by his heterodoxy.

Victor Cousin himself, deprived of institutional power, went into semi-retirement, tantalising Catholics with the prospect of his being received into the Church, though in the event he never took the final step.[2] His retrospective musings on his own career included a demure admission of closeness to Hegel, though he insisted on his philosophical reservations about the philosopher who, in his view, had never quite abandoned the 18th century.[3]

The Catholic view, which dominated the early years of the Second Empire, was that articulated by the Oratorian priest *le père* Alphonse-Joseph Gratry. Gratry was for a time the chaplain at the Ecole Normale, where he purged the library of Hegel and other unsuitable reading matter. He led the attack against Vacherot in 1851, though he also lost his own post in the process. Gratry's mystical eclecticism set him in a central position between liberals and traditionalists in the Catholic community, his writing and preaching were very widely received, and he is often regarded as the most accomplished Catholic philosopher in Second Empire France.[4] Gratry regarded Hegel as pantheist in form and atheist in substance. Not only did he dismiss the religious philosophy as pernicious but he launched a virulent attack on the *Logic*, which he regarded as the basis of Hegel's sophistry.[5]

Pantheism was consequently the major issue in debate on Hegel. Surviving eclectics like Saisset, Janet and Caro were anxious to defend themselves from accusations of pantheism at the same time as defending metaphysics against the rising dominance of positivism. Emile Saisset and Paul Janet were concerned that Hegel's brand of pantheism was too close to atheism for their comfort, making it more difficult for them to defend their own discreet Spinozism.[6] Elme-Marie Caro reproached Hegel with providing powerful arguments against the notion of a

---

[1] See Vacherot, *La Métaphysique et la science ou principes de métaphysique positive*, 1858.

[2] See Margerie, 'V. Cousin et son école', 1867.

[3] See Cousin, 'Une promenade philosophique en Allemagne, Fragmens [sic] d'un journal de voyage, le début et l'épilogue', 1857, and 'Une promenade philosophique en Allemagne', 1866.

[4] See Foucher, *La philosophie catholique en France au XIXe siècle*, 1955, pp.197-236.

[5] See Gratry, *Philosophie: La Logique*, 1855.

[6] See Saisset, *Essais de philosophie religieuse*, 1859; 'Leibnitz et Hegel, d'après de nouveaux documens [sic]', 1860; *Précurseurs et disciples de Descartes*, 1862; and Janet, *Etudes sur la dialectique dans Platon et dans Hegel*, 1860.

personal God. And Emile Beaussire presented an interpretation of the 18th century French materialist Dom Deschamps as an obvious precursor of Hegel who took his philosophy to its logical conclusions in atheism and communism, either of which was sufficient to damn his enterprise.[7] From an anti-metaphysical standpoint, the leading neo-criticist, Charles Renouvier saw Hegel as the guiding light behind attempts to derive a pantheistic religion from positivism.[8]

There is no doubt that some at least of the leading positivists were strongly affected by Hegel. He did not appeal to determined secularists like Emile Littré or Claude Bernard, to be sure. But Comte himself was not entirely impervious, as has been seen. And Hegel exercised a strong attraction on both Taine and Renan, who discovered his work as young men in the late 1840s. Ernest Renan encountered Hegel towards the end of the July Monarchy. Sharing Taine's enthusiasm for Comtean positivism, he attempted to combine it with religion, adapting Hegel's conception of evolution as realisation of the Absolute Idea, and arguing that the task of progress is to bring God into existence.[9] These efforts are reflected in his work, *L'Avenir de la science*, which was written during the Second Republic, though only published in 1890; in his *Dialogues et fragments philosophiques*, written between 1860 and 1871; and in his *Vie de Jésus* (1863), which echoed the Hegelian David Strauss's much reprinted work. Renan was, however, sceptical about metaphysics and rootedly opposed to systematic philosophy. He respected Hegel, and borrowed selectively from him.

Hyppolite Taine was a more enthusiastic systematiser, and as a student espoused the ideas of Spinoza. His philosophy teacher at the Collège Bourbon in 1848-49 was Charles Bénard, the translator of the Aesthetics, who lent Taine copies of Hegel's works, and at the Ecole Normale he encountered the pro-Hegelian Vacherot. Taine was seeking a historical dimension to his rather abstract Spinozist views, and reading Hegel voraciously in the original German, he recognised it as part at least of a solution. His subsequent work was deeply infused with Hegel's ideas, though he did not ultimately accept the dialectic. Daunted by the totalising ambition of Hegelian philosophy, and advised that the University would not accept a thesis which he was contemplating on Hegel's logic, Taine left philosophy for literature, and his 1853 thesis on La Fontaine was a thinly

---

[7] See Beaussire, *Antécédents de l'Hégélianisme dans la philosophie française*, 1865, and Janet, 'Un précurseur français de Hegel, Dom Deschamps', 1865.
[8] See Renouvier, 'De la philosophie du dix-neuvième siècle en France', 1868.
[9] See Charlton, *Positivist Thought in France during the Second Empire 1852-1870*, 1959, pp.86-126.

disguised treatise of Hegelian aesthetics.[10] Taine, like Cousin before him, was subsequently careful to conceal from public view his debt to Hegel, though his writings on the history of ideas, literature and art draw on many Hegelian insights.

The spread of Hegelian aesthetics was not entirely covert, however. Bénard's translations were the only renderings of Hegel to be published by any French scholar,[11] and evidently enjoyed a wide audience, to judge from the full and partial reprintings through which they went.[12] Taine was not the only one to realise that ideas which were stigmatised in their philosophical expression could often be discussed in literary dress. But it is notoriously difficult to trace ideas across disciplinary boundaries, and the presence of Hegelian echoes in literature and criticism poses complex questions of intertextuality. It is well known that writers like Mallarmé and Villiers de l'Isle Adam were avidly discussing Hegel in the 1860s. It is less clear how distinct or decisive his ideas were in shaping their own writing practice.[13] Certainly Hegel was a familiar point of reference in discussions of aesthetic theory.[14]

Apart from Bénard's renderings of the Aesthetics, and a short section from the Logic, the only translations to appear in the 19th century were the work of the Italian Augusto Véra.[15] In other respects too Hegel's public appearance in France in the Second Empire was predominantly ensured by foreigners. Véra was a proselytising Hegelian who provided extensive analysis and commentary with his translations, but also wrote a popular short *Introduction à la philosophie de Hegel* (1855), which probably attracted more readers than the translations themselves. He later published a series of essays applying Hegelian methods to a variety of philosophical questions (1864). It is probable, however, that Véra's work chimed less well with the constricted atmosphere of Parisian philosophy, where his efforts attracted condescension rather than emulation, than with the intellectual environment of Italy, which like England and Germany was beginning to experience a Hegelian revival. Echoes of these developments did appear in French in surveys of Italian philosophy by Raffaele Mariano (1867) and Luigi Ferri (1869), who both emphasised the

---

[10] See Evans, *Taine, essai de biographie intérieure*, 1975, pp.205-228; and Giraud, *Essai sur Taine*, 1912, pp.33-41. Later editions of *La Fontaine et ses fables* were radically rewritten to eliminate much of the Hegelian language.

[11] The Wallon and Sloman *Logique subjective* (1854), may be a partial exception, though Sloman at least was English.

[12] See Chapter 2 and bibliography.

[13] See Reynolds, 'Mallarmé and Hegel: Speculation and the Poetics of Reflection', 1991 for a subtle discussion of the relationship between Hegel and Mallarmé. See also Derrida in *Hegel et la pensée moderne*, 1970.

[14] See Levêque, *La Science du beau*, 1861.

[15] See Chapter 2 and bibliography for full details.

role of Véra, described by Mariano as the Apostolus gentium of Hegelianism.

The German Hegelian revival was represented by the veteran Karl-Ludwig Michelet in short articles,[16] and by the German Right-Hegelian Christian Bartholmèss, who had his book on the philosophy of religion published in French (1855). He argued that Hegel's philosophy of religion contained valuable elements for Christian aplogetics provided it could be dissociated from the materialist implications which Young Hegelians like Feuerbach had drawn from it. Feuerbach's *Essence du christianisme* was itself translated into French in 1864.

These publications attracted a polite but muted welcome from liberal and eclectic philosophers like Emile Saisset, Auguste Laugel and Edmond Scherer, who reviewed them in the *Revue des deux mondes*.[17] While recognising the value of certain Hegelian ideas, they were all careful to distance themselves from them. Scherer's comments were particularly influential in the 1860s, and encouraged a mild resurgence of academic interest in Hegel. He saw Véra as the last of the Hegelians, and an overenthusiastic one at that, but considered that Hegel's thought, though difficult and fundamentally flawed, set out some salutary principles. These included the notion that the world was intelligible, which made science and philosophy meaningful; the concept of contradiction and the relativity of truth, which promoted intellectual tolerance; and the importance of movement and relation, which supported an account of historical change, even if it did not necessarily all amount to progress.

From the early 1850s, German philosophy was kept under review by journals such as the Catholic *Le Correspondant*,[18] and the *Revue des deux mondes*,[19] who were both keenly aware that the struggles between the Right Hegelians and the followers of Schelling and Schopenhauer were closely bound up with the political battles in post-1848 Germany. The monitoring of German philosophy by France's Germanists served both to maintain awareness of the revival of Hegel's ideas in that country and also

---

[16] See Michelet, 'Esquisse de logique', 1856, and 'L'hégélianisme en 1867', 1868.

[17] See Saisset, 'La philosophie moderne depuis Ramus jusqu'à Hegel', 1856, 'Leibnitz et Hegel, d'après de nouveaux documens [sic]', 1860; Laugel, Untitled review, 1859; and Scherer, 'Hegel et l'hégélianisme', 1861.

[18] See Darboy, 'Théorie et pratique de la nouvelle philosophie allemande', 1854, and Eckstein, 'Essai d'une philosophie de l'histoire par le baron Barchou de Penhoën', 1854.

[19] See Taillandier, 'La littérature en Allemagne depuis la Révolution de février', 1850, and 'Le mouvement littéraire de l'Allemagne', 1853.

to emphasise their Prussian associations.[20] Augustin Marrast's useful summary of Hegel's *Philosophy of Right* (1869) was accompanied by sniping remarks about German fascination with their own State apparatus. And those who read Michelet's appraisal of Hegelianism in 1867 will not have been very surprised to see the Berlin philosopher conclude, with evident approval, that 'the victorious armies of Prussia have pressed forward, on the ends of their bayonets, ideas which will soon penetrate into reality'.[21] The French had always been wary of the German military-philosophical complex, and its penetration into reality was to prove extremely unpleasant. That is probably why the Hegel Centenary of 1870 was such a muted affair in France, and the appeal by Renan, Taine and Janet for subscriptions towards a commemorative statue in Berlin aroused so little enthusiasm.[22]

The centenary came at a time of incipient revival for Hegelian thought in England, Italy and Germany. But it could not have come at a worse time for France, since the summer of 1870 was marked by the victorious advance of the Prussian armies into France, the defeat of Sedan and the siege of Paris. Hegel's centenary was reported rather than celebrated in France. Emile Beaussire wondered 'what can ideas be worth which need to be consecrated in the blood of thousands of reasonable beings and in the ruin of a great nation'.[23] Acknowledging the intellectual force of Hegel's thought, he considered that 'Hegel's objective idealism is nationalistic and bellicose' and promotes 'the universal domination of Germany'.[24] He did not think it would ever find favour in France. Renouvier took the same view, interestingly suggesting a link between objective idealism and authoritarian political structures, whereas he saw a subjective stance as more appropriate to a Republic.[25] Between them they came not to praise Hegel but to bury him, for with their comments he was consigned to two decades of virtual oblivion in the French University.

---

20   See articles by Dantier (1856), Nefftzer (1858), Dolfuss (1858), Foucher de Careil (1862), Weber (1866), Nourrisson (1867).

21   Michelet, 'L'hégélianisme en 1867', 1868, p.143.

22   See Taine & Renan, Untitled article, 1870.

23   Beaussire, 'Le centenaire de Hegel en 1870', 1871, p.146.

24   Beaussire, 'La philosophie politique de Hegel, à l'occasion de son centenaire', 1871, p.202.

25   See Renouvier, 'La doctrine hégélienne et la politique prussienne', 1872.

CHAPTER FOUR
HEGEL DURING THE FIRST PART OF THE
THIRD REPUBLIC 1870-1914

The long silence which enveloped Hegel in France after 1870 was primarily due to the humiliation of defeat in war. It was also compounded by the root and branch eradication of the French socialist movement which followed the massacre of the Commune. Hegel's associations with revolution combined with the resurgence of Catholic *intégrisme* were further motivators in the matter. The Véra translations continued to appear and were even reprinted, but in public at least Hegel was at best relegated to being just another episode in the history of philosophy. He was broached respectfully but critically in the Alsacien Alfred Weber's broader survey of European philosophy, written before the *débâcle*, but much reprinted.[1] Thereafter he was generally attacked as a German sophist, recalling the slur which *le père* Gratry had attempted to launch. Pierre-Auguste Bertauld wrote in 1871 that 'nothing could be more empty or meaningless than this long string of pedantic nonsense called Hegel's *Logic*'.[2]   And for the next sixteen years, no French scholar produced any discussion of substance on Hegel. It is true that several relevant translations appeared during the late 1870s. These were mainly histories of philosophy,[3] but they also included Karl Marx's masterwork, *Le Capital* (1872-75), with its prefatory acknowledgement of the Hegelian dialectic, and Friedrich Engels's influential popular account of socialist thought and its origins in Hegelian philosophy (1880). These last two works betokened the future importance of the socialist movement in rehabilitating Hegel in France. At the same time, Charles Bénard discreetly maintained the presence of Hegelian aesthetics by a second edition of his translation (1875), and by an essay on contemporary German aesthetics (1876).

Otherwise the long silence was broken only in 1887 with a review of Hegel's correspondance, newly published in the German Collected

---

[1] See Weber, *Histoire de la philosophie européenne*, 1871.

[2] Bertauld, *De la méthode. Introduction à la recherche des causes premières*, vol. 1, 1876, p.310.

[3] See Zeller, *La Philosophie des Grecs*, 1877; Flint, *La Philosophie de l'histoire en France et Allemagne*, 1878; Stahl, *Histoire de la Philosophie du Droit*, 1880.

Works, and a vitriolic denunciation by Théodore Funck-Brentano. He fulminated against Hegel as an example of German sophistry whose work led straight to the socialists, communists and anarchists whom he denounced as Russian nihilists.[4] Soon afterwards, Lucien Lévy-Bruhl published discussions of Hegel's political theory, which related to the development of German national awareness.[5] And from that time forward, Hegel was readmitted into the University, hesitantly at first, but securely enough to merit a slow but steady flow of learned articles, theses and chapters devoted to his work in various areas of philosophy.

Of course, the French University of the Third Republic was in many respects a different institution from its Royal and Imperial predecessors, especially after the ideological cease-fire which followed the amnesty of the *communards*, and after the reforming work of Jules Ferry in the Ministry of Education had begun to bear fruit. No longer bound by the constraints of respect for, if not conformity with, Catholic teaching, the expanding education system began to accommodate elements of the radical and socialist movements which had previously been excluded. As a result, there was by the early 1890s a new generation of socialist-minded intellectuals, who even before the Dreyfus affair were combining academic explorations with political involvement.

Most influential in the academic community was the Alsatian Germanist, Lucien Herr, who was the librarian at the Ecole Normale from 1886, and a founder with Jaurès of the French Socialist Party.[6] He wrote the article on Hegel for the prestigious *Grande Encyclopédie* which is often credited with having rehabilitated the philosopher in France (1893-4). Rejecting the caricature of Hegel's subservience to the Prussian state, he signalled the importance of the *Phenomenology of Mind* as an introduction to Hegelian philosophy, and of the *Science of Logic* as the key to his system. Unfortunately, neither were available in French, and Herr issued a warning against the unreliable Véra translations with their 'overabundant and mediocre commentaries'.[7] He recognised that Hegel's ideas were dead as systematic doctrine, but thought they were very much alive as underlying tendencies. Herr never wrote the book on Hegel which he planned, but he passed on his interest to many socialist *normaliens*, including Jean Jaurès and later Léon Blum.

---

4 See Funck-Brentano, *Les sophistes allemands et les nihilistes russes*, 1887.

5 See Lévy-Bruhl, *La Théorie de l'Etat dans Hegel*, 1889, and *L'Allemagne depuis Leibniz, essai sur la conscience nationale en Allemagne, 1700-1848*, 1890.

6 See Lindenberg, *Le Marxisme introuvable*, 1975, pp.125-173. Herr is also credited with suggesting the name *L'Humanité* for the socialist (later communist) daily paper.

7 Herr, 'Hegel', 1893-94, p.1002.

No doubt the most important representative of the new generation, historically, was Jean Jaurès. Though five years older than Herr, he learned a great deal from him at the Ecole Normale, and it was Herr who led him to espouse the cause of socialism. As a complementary thesis for his doctorate, and therefore written in Latin, he analysed the origins of the German socialist movement (1892), including an extensive study of Hegel's thought. Though he had reservations about what he considered to be a divinisation of the State and a fatalistic conception of progress, Jaurès saw Hegel as the father of German dialectical socialism which in his view converged strikingly with French ethical socialism.

Another Alsatian and socialist, Charles Andler, who lectured at the Ecole Normale, devoted his doctoral thesis to a study of the origins of State socialism in Germany.[8] In it he examined the Hegelian conceptions of Law, Property, Expropriation, Economics, Value and Labour, and traced their development by later Hegelian and socialist thinkers in Germany (Savigny, Gans, Lasalle, Rodbertus, Thünen, List). Though generally antagonistic to Marxist applications of Hegel, Andler was influential in promoting studies on Hegel and socialist theory in the University, especially after the War, when he held a Chair at the Collège de France. He worked closely with another Germanist, Victor Basch, who was prominent in the human rights movement in the wake of the Dreyfus case. Basch was an authority on the thought of Schiller and of the Young Hegelian Max Stirner.[9] He subsequently contributed the chapter on Hegel to the standard account of 19th century German philosophy which Andler edited in 1912. Basch insisted on the progressive practical import of Hegel's political philosophy, while Andler was more fearful of what he saw as its agressive pan-Germanism.

During the 1890s and 1900s socialist publishers presented translations of several works drawing the connexion between their ideas and Hegel. These included Georgi Plekhanov's celebration of the sixtieth anniversary of Hegel's death, Werner Sombart's history of the German socialist movement, Karl Marx's critique of Hegel's *Philosophy of Right*, and Christian Cornélissen's analysis of the Hegelian dialectic in Marx.[10] But perhaps the most influential was the work of the Italian neo-Hegelian Benedetto Croce, whose major studies of aesthetics and

---

[8] See Andler, *Les origines du socialisme d'Etat en Allemagne*, 1897.

[9] See Basch, *La Poétique de Schiller*, 1902, and *L'Individualisme anarchiste, Max Stirner*, 1904.

[10] Plekhanov, 'La philosophie de Hegel', 1894; Sombart, *Le Socialisme et le mouvement social au XIXe siècle*, 1898; Marx, 'Critique de la philosophie du droit de Hegel', 1895; and Cornélissen, 'La dialectique dans l'oeuvre de Marx', 1901.

social theory were highly esteemed by socialist intellectuals in the mould of Jaurès. These added to the growing debates of a period of intense development in French socialism. In the period before the unification of the French Socialist Party under Jaurès in 1905, many different theoretical approaches jostled for attention, and not all French socialists were equally enthusiastic about the rediscovery of Hegelian origins. In 1895, for example, Marx's son-in-law Paul Lafargue attacked Jaurès for attempting to synthesise Marxist materialism with Hegelian idealism and emphasised that Marx had developed his theory by instituting a radical break with the Hegelian system.[11] It was a debate which has continued to exercise socialist writers, especially in the Marxist tradition. However, the price of socialist unity was the burying of theoretical differences, and after the formation of the new, united French socialist party in 1905 the level of intellectual reflection, like the vigour of debate, fell sharply. Hegelian ideas remained relatively little studied and less understood in the French socialist tradition, but they had nonetheless found a niche again in French thought, and the looming figure of Hegel as the intellectual father of Marx began to take shape.

Outside the socialist milieu, interest in Hegel slowly emerged again in the 1890s from the long sleep. It was prodded partly by the socialist activity, partly by the strong Hegelian revival in Germany, Italy and England, and partly by the resurgence in spiritualist and metaphysical philosophy within the University. The *Revue de métaphysique et de morale*, founded in 1893, articulated the new centre of gravity of Republican intellectual life, displacing the more patrician *Revue des deux mondes*. Carrying its radical-socialist leanings lightly,[12] it echoed the English neo-Hegelian revival led by MacTaggart,[13] and reflected socialist interest in Hegel through Andler and later Georges Sorel.[14] It also commissioned a major study of Hegel's *Logic*, which appeared in some seven instalments from 1894 to 1896, before being published in volume form. Its author, Georges Noël, intended it not only as a scrupulous scholarly discussion, which it was, but also as a counterblast to the positivism and post-Kantian neo-criticism which were still powerful forces in French philosophy. Noël considered that historically Hegel represented the highest achievement of philosophy, as yet still not transcended by any successor. While this work remained the standard study of Hegel's *Logic* for decades, Noël died a short while after completing it, and few were inclined to share his enthusiasm for Hegel. Ten years later, his achievement was acknowledged at a session

---

11   Lafargue (1895).

12   The term 'radical' is used here to designate the French political tendency of that name, which was a centrist republican movement.

13   See MacTaggart, 'Du vrai sens de la dialectique de Hegel', 1893.

14   See Andler, 'La conception matérialiste de l'histoire d'après M. Antonio Labriola', 1897; Sorel, 'Vues sur les problèmes de la philosophie', 1910.

of the French Philosophy Society, when Emile Boutroux referred to him as the only French Hegelian. Boutroux was responding to a formal paper by René Berthelot who had attempted to rehabilitate Hegel in academic terms, drawing parallels between him and Bergson, whose philosophy was beginning to exercise a strong influence in France.[15] In particular, Berthelot sought to refute what he saw as the misperception of Hegelian philosophy as either an absolute determinism, or an integral optimism, or a form of panlogism, which reduced the world to combinations of concepts. He spoke knowledgeably about the influence of Hegel on Marx, whom he regarded as basically a Left Hegelian, and declared that the revolutionary implications were wholly compatible with Hegelian principles.

In the same year the relation between Marx and Hegel was the specific subject of a doctorate in the Paris Law Faculty.[16] Sharing Berthelot's view of the revolutionary implications of the Hegelian dialectic, Léopold Leseine saw the dialectic as rather a mystificatory element which detracted from a scientific (and deterministic) analysis of society. Initially active on the fringes of the socialist movement, Leseine did not pursue his researches after the abrupt conversion to a traditionalist Catholicism which he underwent soon afterwards.

With the generalised thaw in attitudes to Hegel, there were inklings of Catholic interest in Hegel's philosophy of religion.[17] These were, however, defensive and tentative reponses which preferred to emphasise other sources of inspiration of a more orthodox stamp. On the other hand, spiritualist philosophers rediscovered some of their earlier interest. In his study of Spinoza and his legacy, Victor Delbos devoted a chapter to Hegel, speaking warmly of his philosophy as 'Spinozism enriched by all the gains of German idealism'.[18] He felt Hegel had integrated the main principles of Spinoza's ethics and that his system represented the culmination of German speculative philosophy. A better-known spiritualist of the period, Octave Hamelin, had aspirations to propound a systematic idealism, and imbibed the spirit of Hegel in the process. Though his published work on Greek philosophy fell short of the reputation for bold thinking he enjoyed among his

[15] See Berthelot, 'Thèse: Sur la nécessité, la finalité et la liberté chez Hegel', 1907.
[16] See Leseine, L'Influence de Hegel sur Marx, 1907.
[17] See Amant, 'Une des sources de la pensée moderne: l'évolution du Spinozisme', 1894; Denis, 'De l'influence de la philosophie de Kant et de celle de Hegel sur la critique historique appliquée aux origines chrétiennes', 1900; Grégoire de Tours, 'Hegel et saint Bonaventure', 1904; Coutan, 'Note sur l'absolu et Dieu à propos de la philosophie hégélienne', 1912.
[18] Delbos, Le problème moral dans Spinoza et dans l'histoire du Spinozisme, 1893, p.444.

peers, his posthumously published thesis on Descartes had some success in presenting a Hegelianised view of the latter as a systematic idealist.[19]

At last, in 1912, the first French popularisation of Hegel's life and work appeared. Paul Roques's very substantial and informative introduction drew extensively on original manuscripts and German editions. He presented a biographical approach to the subject, intercalating detailed discussion of individual works as they occurred chronologically. Recognising that there had been a slight increase of interest in Hegel, albeit from a very low starting point, Roques suggested that there was scope for seeing Hegel's synthetic approach as complementary to the analytical approach of the more fashionable positivist and empiricist outlooks. Characteristically for serious work on Hegel, Roques was a Germanist, and the book was a culmination of long study in Berlin. It also appeared at a most inauspicious moment, as Europe was preparing for war, and as France was gearing up for hostilities against Germany. The vain struggle of the peace movement was symbolised by the assassination of Jaurès on the eve of war. The combination of anti-German patriotism with the submergence of the socialist movement in the grand coalition of national unity ensured that Hegel once more disappeared from French intellectual life, or at least from its public expression.

---

[19] See Hamelin, *Le système de Descartes*, 1911.

CHAPTER FIVE
HEGEL IN THE INTERWAR PERIOD

The Great War did not produce the kind of prolonged silence over Hegel which had followed the Franco-Prussian war. No doubt the defeat of Germany made its thinkers appear less threatening. No doubt too, the associations with revolution, which had long dogged Hegel in French eyes, now attached themselves to Marx and Lenin rather than to classical German philosophy. And while some socialists at least continued to count Hegel among their forebears, Hegel's reputation increasingly acquired the political elbow-room in which it could grow and diversify.

In the 1920s, discussion of Hegel was largely confined to works of academic philosophy. Victor Basch and Charles Andler remained influential in the centre-left socialist current of the University, though Hegel was a small part of their preoccupations.[1] Close to them intellectually was the distinguished philosopher of science, Emile Meyerson. His major work on scientific rationality, *De l'explication dans les sciences* (1921) drew heavily on Hegelian concepts, which he used to develop explanatory approaches based on the fundamental unity of reason, even if that unity was antinomial in nature. Meyerson recognised Hegel's gigantic achievement and regarded it as a powerful resource in his attack on positivistic resistance to an integrated philosophy of science. Meyerson's enthusiasm was not shared by the mainstream, anti-metaphysical current of academic philosophy. His Sorbonne colleague Léon Brunschvicg, a member of the critical idealist school, opposed the metaphysical tendencies of Hegelianism in his influential book *Le progrès de la conscience dans la philosophie occidentale* (1927), while recognising Hegel's historical stature.

On the Catholic side of the University, there was a gradual awakening of interest in Hegel, viewed as a philosopher of religion. The impetus for this re-evaluation of an old enemy came in part from the collapse of Catholic *intégrisme* after the Great War. It was symbolised by the banning of the Right-wing Action française, and provoked a search for new political and intellectual frameworks within which to articulate

---

[1] See Basch, *Les Doctrines politiques des philosophes classiques de l'Allemagne*, 1927.

Christian faith. Hegel's slow rehabilitation with Catholics was probably prompted by the leading historian of philosophy Emile Bréhier. A pupil of Henri Bergson, whose vitalist philosophy offered many points of contact with Catholic thought, Bréhier saw Hegel as transposing the Christian religion into philosophy.[2] In his view, Hegel's thought could best be understood through his early preoccupations with religion, and should be seen as a 'speculative and philosophical interpretation of Christianity',[3] even though it had frequently been resisted in Christian circles. In 1927, Bréhier founded a journal, *Revue d'histoire de la philosophie*, which in the late 1920s and early 1930s published several important studies of Hegel.[4] They included, among others, Alexandre Koyré's much-quoted survey of Hegel studies in France (1931) and part of Jean Wahl's seminal work on the unhappy consciousness in Hegel. The journal's publishers, Gamber, also published two important doctoral theses by the Romanian philosopher D. D. Rosca, in 1928. The longer one was an examination of Hegel's influence on Hyppolite Taine, especially in the field of aesthetics. The shorter was a translation of one of Hegel's early works, *La Vie de Jésus*, with a substantial introduction emphasising its spiritual and theological importance.

It was indicative of the new mood that the christian-democratic philosopher Paul Archambault should publish a popular introduction to Hegel and anthology of texts (1927). But undoubtedly the most significant event in the swelling current of religious interpretations of Hegel was the appearance of Jean Wahl's study of 1929, *Le Malheur de la conscience dans la philosophie de Hegel*. Wahl insisted that it was necessary to look beneath the often rather rigid systematic philosophy of the later Hegel to see it as a development of the spiritual and emotional impulse which appears with such clarity in the early works. For Wahl, the dialectic was an experience and an intuition before it was elaborated into conceptual terms, and the theological inspiration of Hegel's initial project suffused his entire work. He saw the *Phenomenology* as the key text, and in particular he focused on the analysis of the moment of 'unhappy consciousness', when in Hegel's account the conscious self becomes aware of its divided and contradictory nature, prior to attaining unity through the ministry of a mediator. The theological import of this analysis is clearly linked with a characteristically protestant (or Jansenist) doctrine of the redemption by Christ of fallen humanity. There are echoes of Pascal, whose tercentenary had just been vigorously marked, and of Kierkegaard, to whom Wahl next turned his attention,[5] and with whom Wahl considered Hegel had deep and subtle affinities. At the same time as he instituted a new view of Hegel,

---

2 See Bréhier, *Histoire de la philosophie allemande*, 1921.
3 Bréhier, *Histoire de la philosophie allemande*, p.130.
4 These included articles by Sée (1927), Wahl (1927-28), Tchijéwsky (1929), Koyré (1931), and Lenoir (1931). Details are given in the appended bibliography.
5 See Wahl, *Etudes kierkegaardiennes*, 1938.

Wahl laid Hegelian foundations both for a rejuvenated theology and for a nascent existentialist movement. It was a remarkable achievement, though one which has commonly been overshadowed by the work of his neo-hegelian and existentialist successors.

Outside the University, there were writers, especially poets, who looked to Hegel. Paul Valéry's quest for an intellectual universality and his austere poetic exploration of the moments of consciousness have distinctly Hegelian echoes, and he may perhaps have inherited some of Mallarmé's fascination with the philosopher. More overtly, the surrealist movement of the 1920s looked to Hegel as a possible means of connecting their discovery of the Freudian unconscious with political and social development. André Breton immersed himself in Hegel's dialectic in the hope of learning how irreconcilable antinomies could be transcended.[6] He concluded, however, that Hegel's great systematic edifice had to be rejected in order to recover the experiential authenticity at its heart. Close to the surrealists in some respects, dissident young Marxist intellectuals began to rediscover Marx's early philosophical and therefore Hegelian preoccupations. Among them were former surrealists like Georges Friedmann and Pierre Naville, as well as young philosophers like Henri Lefebvre and Georges Politzer. Groups gathered around small-circulation and short-lived journals such as *La Revue marxiste*, *Philosophies*, and *Avant-poste*, which latter published the first French translations from Marx's 1844 Paris Manuscripts, which popularised the Hegelian-Marxist concept of alienation.[7]

1930 was the centenary of Hegel's death, and the occasion for a plethora of commemorations and reevaluations of Hegel on an international scale,[8] throughout Europe and in the Soviet Union and Japan. The first International Hegel Congress was held in the Hague and was the occasion for reports on the influence of Hegel in several European countries. Alexandre Koyré presented a survey of Hegel in France which argued that with a small number of exceptions, including himself, Basch, Andler and Meyerson, Hegel had largely been neglected in France.[9] Among the possible reasons, he cited anti-German feeling as well as philosophical opposition from Catholics, positivists and neo-Kantians. He did however, see Jean Wahl's work as pointing to a renewal of interest. Koyré's analysis has been widely quoted, and some scholars have over-

---

[6]   This is usefully documented in Bernard-Paul, Robert, *Antécédents du surréalisme*, Presses Universitaires d'Ottawa, 1988.

[7]   See Marx, 'Critique de la dialectique hégélienne', 1933.

[8]   According to Steinhauer, the number of publications worldwide on Hegel reached a prewar peak of 334 in 1931, more than three times as many as the previous three years put together.

[9]   See Koyré, 'Rapport sur l'état des études hégéliennes en France', 1931.

hastily taken it to indicate that France ignored Hegel entirely before 1930.[10]

At the same time, in France, two of the leading journals in French academic philosophy published special issues to mark the centenary. The *Revue de métaphysique et de morale* (1931) published six substantial essays, including translated pieces by Benedetto Croce and Nicolai Hartmann. The journal's centre-left orientation was reflected in articles by Victor Basch on the *Phenomenology* and Charles Andler on the *Aesthetics* as well in René Berthelot's examination of Hegel's relations with Goethe and Edmond Vermeil's lengthy exposition of Hegel's political theory. The *Revue philosophique*, which during the 1920s had carried several articles on Hegel by Jean Wahl and the Dutch socialist Bernard Groethuysen,[11] marked the centenary with articles by Basch, Koyré and Wahl, the latter drawing links between Hegel and Kierkegaard.

The 1930s were a busy decade for the exploration of Hegel in France. With deceptive naturalness, Hegel loomed larger in the histories of philosophy, such as those produced by Alain (1932) and Emile Bréhier (1932), and was a frequent subject of articles in the main philosophical reviews. Following Wahl's lead, much of the discussion focused on the *Phenomenology* and on Hegel's early works, with their religious preoccupations.[12] These attracted the participation of Jesuit philosophers like Henri Rondet and Aimé Forest who, from within the Thomist movement, were attempting to reappraise the possible applications of a philosophy which the Church had condemned in the 19th century. Although the *Phenomenology* was still unavailable in French, extracts had appeared, several commentaries were available, and Jean Hyppolite was known to be preparing his major translation, which appeared in 1939 and 1941. Less remarked at the time, though subsequently influential, was a series of seminars at the Ecole Pratique des Hautes Etudes on the philosophy of religion. Given by Alexandre Kojevnikoff (later Kojève), a Russian émigré who had studied in Germany, they consisted of a reading of the *Phenomenology* focused on the Master-Slave relationship. The documents were not published until after the war, and though the seminar was sparsely attended, those who were marked by it included several figures who became prominent in the postwar period. Among them were the philosopher Maurice Merleau-Ponty, the surrealist André Breton, the psychoanalyst Jacques Lacan, the political theorist Raymond Aron, the

---

[10] See Poster, *Existential Marxism*, 1975; and Roth, *Knowing and History*, 1988.
[11] See Wahl's articles of 1926 and 1927; and Groethuysen's of 1923 and 1925.
[12] See Koyré, 'Hegel à Jena. A propos de publications récentes', 1934; Hyppolite, 'Les travaux de jeunesse de Hegel d'après des ouvrages récents', 1935, and 'Vie et prise de conscience de la vie dans la philosophie hégélienne d'Jéna', 1938; and Rondet, 'Hegel et le christianisme, réflexions théologiques', 1936.

theologian Gaston Fessard, and writers Georges Bataille and Raymond Queneau, who supervised the publication of Kojève's readings from notes and other materials.[13] Beginning from a religious approach to Hegel, Kojeve's analysis of consciousness and its relation to the world converged with aspects of phenomenological thought which were fundamental to the emerging existentialist movement.

Following hard on the heels of the religious rediscovery of Hegel came the rediscovery of the Hegelian origins of Marxism, particularly by the young generation of communist intellectuals. An immediate spur to reflection was the appearance for the first time of Marx's Paris Manuscripts of 1844, and the republication of Marx's other early philosophical writings, largely concerned with discussion of Hegel and the Young Hegelians, and all heavily imbued with Hegelian concepts of consciousness and alienation. Henri Lefebvre and Norbert Guterman were active in translating and popularising these writings, and drew on them in their book *La conscience mystifiée* (1936). They examined the Hegelian concepts discussed by Wahl, but pointed to the social roots of alienated consciousness and to political rather than religious solutions. They subsequently translated extensive extracts from Hegel's work,[14] and Lenin's notes on Hegel,[15] drawing attention to the high value Lenin placed on the dialectical reasoning which he found there. Lefebvre considered that the structures of the Hegelian dialectic could be substantially adopted as Marxist methodology, and in his influential book *Le Matérialisme dialectique* (1939) he traced Marx's thought as a development from abstract Hegelian concepts to a concrete dialectical humanism.

An influential work in this direction was Auguste Cornu's doctoral thesis, supervised by Charles Andler, on Marx's early life and work.[16] Cornu saw the early Hegelian and Feuerbachian philosophical writings as steps on the way to mature Marxism, which was thus the logical outcome of classical German philosophy. His careful historical analysis did more to promote a Hegelianised Marx than any proselytising might have done. As a consequence, the early Marx was much better known in France than the later Marx, and the problem of his relation to Hegel was correspondingly magnified in importance. Cornu's work was widely read and the progressive Catholic review *Esprit* published a lengthy series of reflections on it, which further stimulated religious interest in Hegel.[17] Other Marxist intellectuals took up the questions, taking care to emphasise that Marx had 'inverted' Hegel's idealist dialectic to achieve a materialist

---

[13] See Kojève, *Introduction à la lecture de Hegel*, 1947.
[14] *Morceaux choisis*, 1939.
[15] See Lénine, *Cahiers sur la dialectique de Hegel*, 1938.
[16] See Cornu, *Karl Marx, l'homme et l'oeuvre*, 1934.
[17] See Moré, 'Les années d'apprentissage de Karl Marx. A propos d'un livre récent', 1935-36.

dialectic.[18] The rapid growth of interest in Marxist philosophy during the 1930s ensured that the question of Hegel remained posed, despite the subsequent attempts of Stalin and his enforcers to insist that it had been solved.

As the 1930s ended, the French Hegelian revival was in full swing, with the appearance of substantial new translations, including for the first time the *Phenomenology of Mind*, the *Philosophy of Right*, and the *Philosophy of History*. To a large extent the national, political and religious grounds for objection to his work had been dissolved. Hegel had in a sense become naturalised in France, and his German origins provoked few inhibitions. It seemed, for example, appropriate that, despite the virtual inevitability of war with Germany, the *Revue philosophique* should mark the 150th anniversary of the French Revolution with two articles on Hegel and 1789. Similarly, Hegel had become politically plural. To be sure, his relation to Marx was strongly perceived, but socialists of all hues from communists to radical-socialists and Left Catholics were studying him with enthusiasm, and he was attracting interest from traditionally conservative Catholic quarters. The religious objections to his pantheism and crypto-atheism had not wholly vanished, but there was a growing awareness that his work could offer much to an exploration of religious experience and perhaps also to systematic theology.

By the outbreak of war, Hegel's 'Long March' in France was at an end. The seeds which were germinating in the 1930s flowered at the Liberation. The intermittent and fragile history of Hegel's reception in France spanned more than a century before he was finally accepted as one of the 'three Hs' dominating French thought.[19] But by the same token this history ceased to be unitary. There were many complex links between the phenomenologists, the Marxists and the Catholics who looked to Hegel, and a complex relationship between them and the University, where a growing number of scholars turned on Hegel an academic interest which eschewed explicit political or ideological affiliations. So the history of Hegel in France must henceforward be written in the plural, and the second part of this study will address several different conceptions of Hegel with their different histories.

---

[18] See *A la lumière du marxisme*, 1935.
[19] This expression is used by Descombes in his *Le Même et l'autre*, 1979, referring to Hegel, Husserl and Heidegger.

CHAPTER SIX
HEGEL AND PHENOMENOLOGY

The postwar Hegel revival has often been evoked.[1] Its contours are well mapped and familiar, at least in so far as they include the discovery of key aspects of Hegel's *Phenomenology of Mind* by the leading intellectuals of the period, through the agency of Jean Hyppolite and Alexandre Kojève. It will be apparent from the preceding chapters that the history leading up to the revival is longer and more complex than is commonly recognised. It will also be apparent from later chapters that the revival was wider and more enduring than the dominance of the 'generation of the three H's'.[2] However, there can be no doubt that it was the impact of Hegel on existentialist and phenomenological currents of thought that caught the attention and imagination of the postwar Parisian intelligentsia and the international intellectual community after it.

Existentialism was the media event of the Liberation period. The cafés, lecture theatres and meeting halls of the Latin Quarter were the privileged stage upon which the ideas and images of the movement were played out. Intellectually, it was centred on Jean-Paul Sartre and his circle, but around its periphery were many groups and individuals who claimed an interest in consciousness, anguish, alienation, human freedom or existence.[3]

Existentialism was itself part of a broader movement of ideas and values, given impetus by the mood of postwar France. Though there were many divergences of view between the successors of Hegel, Husserl and Heidegger, those who looked for inspiration to the 'three H's' at this period shared a common range of preoccupations and philosophical approaches loosely identifiable as phenomenological.

---

[1] Excellent accounts appear in Poster, *Existential Marxism in Postwar France*, 1975; Descombes, *Modern French Philosophy*, 1980; Roth, *Knowing and History*, 1988.

[2] See Descombes, *Modern French Philosophy*, p.9.

[3] For a helpful recent account, see David E. Cooper, *Existentialism*, Oxford, Blackwell, 1990, ix-201pp.

Alexandre Kojève's prewar seminars at the Ecole Pratique des Hautes Etudes have already been mentioned.[4] Their impact was to introduce Hegel's *Phenomenology*, and a particular reading of it, to an important section of the young intellectual elite. After the Liberation, Kojève's prewar work attained a much wider audience and a remarkable degree of celebrity with the publication in 1947 of his *Introduction à la lecture de Hegel*. This work, edited by Raymond Queneau, was a compilation of published and unpublished texts by Kojève, summaries of his courses, and students' lecture notes. Dominating the whole was his introductory explication of the passage in the *Phenomenology* dealing with lordship and bondage. The Master-Slave relationship ('Maître-Esclave' as the French version has it) became not only the key to understanding Hegel, but also a fundamental figure in French postwar thought.

Briefly, the Master and Slave are presented by Hegel as the two conflicting and complementary paths which an individual may follow to attain self-awareness through recognition by the consciousness of the Other. For the Master, the desire for recognition is stronger than the fear of death, and, asserting his own independence, he secures dominion over the Slave, who fears death and prefers to opt for life even at the price of submission and dependence on the Master. Paradoxically, the Master's quest for recognition and self-confirmation fails because the Slave has lost the independence necessary to supply it, and the Master also becomes dependent on the Slave's work to provide his life needs. Conversely the Slave learns self-awareness and self-mastery in his fear of the Master and his service to him, and the Slave's work brings him into a perhaps painful but also direct and satisfying relationship with the material world, from which the Master is shielded.[5]

In Kojève's hands the Hegelian analysis became a paradigm for human existence, with application at many levels. Since human reality is fundamentally social, he argued, the Master-Slave relationship is both a necessary form of any person's self-consciousness, and also a necessary pattern of social relations, which are inevitably structured in terms of dependency. Drawing the connection with Marxist political analysis, Kojève saw the Slave as a metaphor for the proletariat, who were at present subjugated but whose very oppression provided the means and the incentive to overcome it. In his view, the way of the Master was historically a dead end, while the way of the Slave affirmed the value of

---

[4] See previous chapter
[5] See Hegel, *Phenomenology of Spirit*, tr. A. V. Miller, Oxford University Press, 1977, paragraphs 178-196, pp.111-119.

Life and Work and offered a prospect for human development, through the struggle to transform the world.[6]

The combination of Heideggerian and Marxist insights in Kojève's reading of Hegel helped it to mesh closely with the preoccupations of postwar France. It was widely adopted as a cogent and decisive analysis, even by those who did not share the further implications Kojève drew from it. One implication was an apocalytic conception of bloody revolution, since Violence was in his view a necessary concomitant of Reason. Another implication was his insistence that History had come to an end, since humanity's only remaining task was to flesh out in detail and implement in full the final shape of its social and intellectual order, which was now known in principle, thanks to Hegel, and already established in practice in the world's leading states.

After the war, Kojève himself intervened in open philosophical debate only intermittently, since he had accepted a senior appointment in the Ministry of Finance. His substantial postwar work was mostly published after his death in 1968, and has attracted the attention of scholars rather than acolytes.[7] But many important figures drew on Kojève's reading of Hegel, not least those who had attended his prewar seminar. Writers Raymond Queneau and Georges Bataille were publicly declared disciples, Queneau having edited Kojève's *Introduction*. And the psychoanalyst Jacques Lacan slipped many an allusion into his seminars, where figures from the *Phenomenology* like the Master-Slave relation and the 'Beautiful Soul' were frequently invoked in his analyses.[8] Lacan diverged from Hegel, however, in insisting on the opacity of desire, its failure to coincide with the conscious subject, which was itself problematised. He argued strongly that psychoanalytical repression could not be understood on the model of Hegelian negation, which simultaneously affirms what it negates, and thus prepares to recover it in a subsequent 'Aufhebung'.[9]

Perhaps closest to Kojève intellectually was the German-born political philosopher Eric Weil, a close contemporary, who also attended the celebrated seminar. Weil's best-known work is his much reprinted *Hegel et l'état* (1950) which presents a closely argued defence of Hegel's theory of the state, concluding that the very fact of being able finally to understand the modern state was a sign that it was close to its end, ready to be superseded by new forms. In his other works, Weil

---

6 See Kojève, *Introduction à la lecture de Hegel*, 1947, especially the opening section 'En guise d'introduction', pp.11-34.
7 There is a valuable discussion of it in Roth, *Knowing and History*, 1988.
8 See Lacan, *Ecrits*, 1966.
9 This issue is argued in some detail in Butler, *Subjects of Desire*, 1987.

developed the search for meaning implicit in the Hegelian philosophy of history. He recognised that both history and philosophy posed serious and perhaps even insuperable obstacles to the quest for meaning. In part this was because he saw history, like politics, as a domain of inherent uncertainty, and in part because he refused to envisage the integration of Violence and Reason. Ultimately Weil turned from Hegel to a Kantian ethic which posed meaning as an article of faith rather than a work of reason.

Jean Hyppolite was the most energetic and influential proponent of neo-Hegelianism throughout the postwar period until his death in 1968. He held powerful positions in the University, and was instrumental in placing Hegel on the *agrégation* syllabus from 1950 onwards, thus ensuring that Hegel became a central feature of philosophy teaching and research in France. He eventually succeeded Merleau-Ponty in the philosophy Chair at the Collège de France.

Hyppolite's approach to Hegel was more self-effacing than Kojève's. Where the latter unrepentantly used Hegel as a vehicle for his own preoccupations, Hyppolite attempted to let Hegel speak for himself, and much of his work took the form of careful exegesis of the Hegelian texts. His weighty doctoral thesis, *Genèse et structure de la Phénoménologie de l'Esprit de Hegel*, was published in 1946 and though it took the form of an academic commentary it proposed what one critic has called a 'heroic Hegelianism',[10] which affirmed the need and the possiblity of making sense of human history.

Hyppolite shared Jean Wahl's view that the 'unhappy consciousness' (rather than the Master-Slave relationship) was the key to understanding Hegel. The divided nature of human consciousness and the pervasiveness of alienation and tragedy in human history were fundamental in Hyppolite's view. They provided the impetus for tension and struggle which, he argued, were the motor of human history and not amenable to resolution either in a Kojèvian End of History or in a Marxian communist society. It was perhaps an ambiguity of Hegel's thought, he suggested, that 'the reconciliation of the subjective spirit and the objective spirit, the supreme synthesis of this system, is perhaps not capable of being carried out in full'.[11]

Much of Hyppolite's writing in the late 1940s was concerned to assert the progressive force of Hegelian philosophy. Never enthusiastic about Marxism, Hyppolite nonetheless recognised the affinities between

---

[10] See Roth, *Knowing and History*, pp.28-40.
[11] Hyppolite, *Introduction à la philosophie de l'histoire de Hegel*, 1948; 1983 edition, p.124.

Marx's early philosophical writings and Hegelian conceptions. He sought to reinstate Hegel's positions against the criticisms Marx had levelled against him, particularly in respect of alienation where he considered Marx over-hasty in supposing that it could be overcome by the movement of history.[12]

During the 1950s, Hyppolite's preoccupation with the meaning of history shifted towards a concern with the logic and structure of historical processes, and eventually towards a predominant attention to the logic and structure of the production of meaning in language. It was this form of neo-Hegelianism that influenced younger philosophers like Michel Serres, Georges Canguilhem and Michel Foucault, and to which the latter paid tribute when he succeeded Hyppolite at the Collège de France.[13] In his later development Hyppolite therefore rejoined the more Heideggerian emphasis on Being common to the existentialists, just as their leading figures were abandoning it for a concern with history.

The dominant figure among the existentialists, Jean-Paul Sartre, had never been an enthusiastic Hegelian, though he was aware in the 1930's of Kojève's seminar, which he did not attend, so far as can be ascertained. In his major work, *L'Etre et le néant* (1943), he acknowledged the power and insight of Hegel's analysis of the Master-Slave relationship, especially in illuminating the complexity of being-for-others. However, he repeatedly returned to criticise Hegel from a Heideggerian perspective. He considered that Hegel had failed to recognise the radical irreducibility of self-consciousness, the impossibility of any subject's adopting the point of view of the totality, the radical separation of Being from Nothing, and the logical priority of Being over Nothing. Moreover, the unity of being *for itself* with being in *itself*, the culminating moment of Hegel's *Phenomenology*, was declared a radical impossibility.

Simone de Beauvoir had considerable respect for Hegel's dialectic. She saw the applicability of the Master-Slave relationship to human relations, especially between men and women, even though his analysis came uncomfortably close to justifying the women's subjugation it described.

However, it was Maurice Merleau-Ponty, among the existentialists, who paid the greatest homage to Hegel, in his often-

---

[12] See Hyppolite, *Etudes sur Marx et Hegel*, 1955, in particular the chapters 'Aliénation et objectivation', pp.82-104; and 'Marxisme et philosophie', pp.107-119.
[13] See Michel Foucault, *L'Ordre du discours*, Paris, Gallimard 1972.

quoted claim that 'Hegel is at the origin of everything great that has been done in philosophy for the past century'.[14] Merleau-Ponty had attended Kojève's seminar in the late 1930s and respected the power and scope of Hegelian philosophy. Since his own phenomenology was less radically dichotomous than Sartre's, he saw the possibility of using Hegel's dialectic to explore the relationship between the individual and society, posed especially in political terms. His reflection on the Soviet show trials, *Humanisme et terreur* (1947), mobilised a Hegelian approach to the relationship between reason and violence to conclude that judgements could only be made in the light of the logic of history. And violence could therefore be legitimate if it served to bring closer a society in which violence would not be necessary. But in his later work, *Les Aventures de la dialectique* (1955), he seriously questioned the Hegelian historicism or Stalinist Marxism which spoke with such apparent confidence of the dialectic of reason and history.

With the notable exceptions of Sartre and Beauvoir, the existentialists and neo-Hegelians moved in the later 1950s towards anti-historicist and anti-humanist positions which owed more to Heidegger than to Hegel. The intellectuals who succeeded them were more concerned with structures of language and discourse than with the meaning of history. Yet they too found it easier to criticise Hegel than to escape from him.

The argument could be made that Hegel had already anticipated, and blocked off, most of the escape routes out of his philosophical system. Since negation and supersession are already such key features of Hegel, it is not difficult to present the attempts to negate or supersede him as in various ways actually confirming him, as being therefore variants of Hegelianism. The point was well made by François Châtelet, who argued that Hegel delimited all the theoretical possibilities of theory, and could not be undermined from within, as 'the Hegelian order admits of no partial *lapsus*: it says what it says, to the point of exhausting meaning'.[15] The return to Nietzsche was in many cases the preferred strategy for securing a radical break which would not subsequently lapse back into Hegel. Gilles Deleuze's ardent espousal of Nietzschean self-affirmation was characteristic of this tendency, André Glucksmann's philosophical guerrilla warfare against totalising master-narratives and Bernard-Henri Lévy's blistering assault on 'the French ideology' were also influential attempts to puncture the Hegelian balloon with a sharp Nietzschean nib.[16]

---

[14] See Merleau-Ponty, 'Une conférence de J. Hyppolite. L'existentialisme chez Hegel', 1945.

[15] Châtelet, *Hegel*, 1968, p.178.

[16] Glucksmann, *Les maîtres penseurs*, 1977, Lévy, *L'Idéologie française*, 1981.

Within the phenomenological tradition, the difficulty and necessity of breaking with Hegel has perhaps been most closely argued by Jacques Derrida. An important part of his deconstruction of the established categories of philosophy has passed through a critical reflection on Hegel, who consequently haunts much of his writing. In one of his earliest works, *L'Ecriture et la différence* (1967), Derrida examined Georges Bataille's adoption of Kojève's reading of Hegel, his struggle with the crushing obviousness of Hegelian categories, and his attempt to avoid being led by the process of 'Aufhebung' to accept Absolute Knowledge, with all its implications of death and finality.[17] In his *Marges de la philosophie* (1972) he examined the complexity of Hegel's relation to humanism and took Hegel's theory of signs as the starting point for a thoroughgoing questioning of the received concepts of writing, language, presence and philosophy.[18]

The most disconcerting of Derrida's works is probably *Glas* (1974), which attempts to confront the pervasive Hegelianism of the most obvious every-day concepts. Texts by several hands, notably Hegel, Genet, and Derrida himself, are confronted on the page in a layout which allows each to interrupt and comment on the others. The work as a whole is a demonstration of the extent to which Hegel has set the framework for modern thought and writing, as well as an attempt to wriggle out of that framework using adventurous textual strategies and devices, for which Derrida has become celebrated.

Among the philosophers whose work owes much to Derrida, Gérard Lebrun has offered one of the most subtle and meticulous approaches to Hegel. He saw Hegelian discourse as ultimately theological, and even as an attempt to constitute a definitive Theology.[19] In a similar vein, Marcel Pacquet concluded that Hegelianism is the ultimate 'logology', and Jean-Luc Nancy traced the site of Hegelian speculative philosophy to the concept of 'Aufhebung', from which 'bon mot' he saw all else following.[20]

The post-structuralist enterprise, of which Derrida is the most challenging exponent, is an interrogation of language and of philosophy, especially of that logocentric enlightenment tradition of which Hegel is the most accomplished representative. The resulting ramification of discourses on discourses or texts on texts strikingly recalls the 'grey in

---

17 Derrida *L'Ecriture et la différence*, 1967, pp.369-407.
18 Derrida, *Marges de la philosophie*, 1972, pp.79-127. There is a useful discussion of this in Christopher Norris, *Derrida*, London, Fontana, 1987, pp.69-77.
19 Lebrun, *La Patience du concept*, 1972.
20 Lebrun, *La Patience du concept*, 1972; Nancy, *La Remarque spéculative*, 1973.

grey' of Hegelian philosophy, and comes near to reproducing the self-development of the concept which lies at the heart of Hegel's gradiose idealist system. Lebrun is not the only writer in post-structuralist circles to have evoked the religious dimensions of Hegel. The Talmudic phenomenology of Emmanuel Lévinas acknowledges debts to Hegel's *Phenomenology*,[21] and has come under recent attention following the rediscovery of Jewish mysticism by Derrida. Nancy's exploration of the limits of language has led him to meditate on the divine. And if the contemporary development of French phenomenology increasingly raises religious questions, it will be an apt reminder of the circumstances in which France first discovered Hegel's *Phenomenology* some sixty years ago, in the Catholic spirituality of Jean Wahl and in the seminars on the philosophy of religion given by Alexandre Kojève.

---

[21] See Seán Hand, editor, *The Levinas Reader*, Oxford, Blackwell, 1989.

CHAPTER SEVEN
HEGEL AND MARXISM

The long association between Hegel and the socialist tradition in France had cut both ways. On the one hand, French socialists and communists could look back to the nineteenth century and see Hegelian ideas in the thought of their predecessors, including figures of the stature of Jaurès, Proudhon and Leroux. On the other hand, each of those predecessors had marked Hegel with their own reservations, whether political, philosophical or religious. And each had also drawn Hegel into the often bitter disputes which have always divided the French Left. The 1905 settlement achieved socialist unity at the cost of stifling theoretical discussion on the Left and inaugurating a philosophical void which lasted for a quarter of a century.

The vigorous emergence of Marxist theory in France during the 1930s took place in the context of a Left bitterly divided between socialists and communists. The socialists still generally preferred to address concrete practical problems rather than abstract theoretical ones, and largely limited their philosophical reflections to ethical questions. Though they acknowledged the interest of Marxist social theory they often looked to the new phenomenological approaches for their philosophy. The communists, on the other hand, attached great importance to ideological struggles, and regarded correct theoretical analysis as the key to effective revolutionary action.

The exploration of Marxist philosophy was pursued energetically by communist intellectuals during the 1930s, resulting in the rediscovery of Marx's early philosophical writings, Lenin's philosophical writings of 1916, and the deeply Hegelian traces which they carried. Henri Lefebvre and Norbert Guterman in particular worked to make the original texts available in French and to draw out their theoretical implications. However, the explorations of intellectuals were shadowed by the construction and imposition of a communist theoretical orthodoxy, Marxism-Leninism, which received its most dogmatic expression in Stalin's notorious *Short Course* on the eve of the Second World War.[1]

The communists were deeply divided by the Molotov-Ribbentrop pact of non-aggression, and the party was banned in France from then until the Liberation. They experienced, however, a spectacular recovery of fortunes at the end of the War, partly because of the communist role in the Resistance, partly because of the Soviet role in the Allied victory, and partly no doubt because of their participation in government (1944-47). The Liberation was a period of intensive activity for those Marxist intellectuals who survived the war, though in many cases their efforts were directed to social reconstruction rather than philosophical investigation. The situation was exacerbated by the lack of printing materials and the absence of books, many of them burnt during the occupation.

In the immediate aftermath of the Liberation, there was a strong tendency among communist intellectuals to emphasise the continuity of Marxism with the great moments in French thought, especially the Enlightenment. Hegel's debt to the *philosophes* was noted in this connection.[2] However, Marx as the successor of Descartes and Diderot was more a product of patriotic enthusiasm than of philosophical enquiry, and soon gave way to the two prewar philosophical tendencies, which coexisted uneasily for a period among Marxists. The first was expressed in the innovative work of Henri Lefebvre, pursued in a series of books, including a short popularisation in the 'Que sais-je?' series,[3] and a formidable treatise on dialectical logic.[4] His earlier volume, *Le Matérialisme dialectique*, was also much reprinted. This short work first appeared during the 'phoney war' but became an influential exposition of Marxist philosophy in the postwar period. Lefebvre saw Marx's thought as a development from Hegel, giving concrete historical content to the abstract Hegelian notions of alienation and the dialectical method. He argued that Hegel's notion of the Absolute Idea at the end of the philosophical process was an abstract form which could be concretely transposed into a Marxian vision of the Whole Man at the end of the historical process. He was also convinced that Marxists could learn a great deal from closer acquaintance with Hegelian logical concepts and categories, all of which were integrated into Marx's own mature thinking. Lefebvre was supported in his reflections by the work of

---

[1] The French translation, *Précis d'Histoire du Parti communiste (bolchévik) de l'URSS*, appeared in early 1939 and sold 300,000 copies before the outbreak of war in September.

[2] See Mougin, 'Hegel et le neveu de Rameau', 1946.

[3] Lefebvre, *Le Marxisme*, 1948.

[4] Lefebvre, *A la lumière du matérialisme dialectique. 1. Logique formelle, logique dialectique*, 1947.

Auguste Cornu, who pursued his scholarly study of Marx's formative years, concentrating on Marx's relations with Hegelian philosophy.[5] Cornu also advocated the reconceptualising of Marxism as a theory of alienation which drew on and developed the insights of Hegel and Feuerbach.[6]

The second philosophical tendency was the more orthodox line adopted by Stalin's *Short Course*. As a simple schema, it had considerable didactic force, reducing dialectics and materialism to four and three main features respectively, and eschewing philosophical complexities and ambiguities. The role of Hegel in the formation of Marx's dialectic was acknowledged, but it was stressed that 'Marx and Engels took from the Hegelian dialectic only its "rational kernel", casting aside its idealistic shell, and developed it further so as to lend it a modern scientific form'.[7] In practice this was generally interpreted as closing the question of Hegel, which thus became only of antiquarian interest.

As the Cold War began to polarise minds and harden subtle distinctions it was the Stalinist line which prevailed. According to Stalin's ideological chief, Andrei Zhdanov, and his French epigone, Laurent Casanova, the problem of Hegel was long settled: Marxism was a radical departure from Hegelian philosophy. Lefebvre and Cornu were both required to write self-criticisms acknowledging the insufficiency of their earlier views, which erred by overstressing the importance of the early Marx, Hegel and alienation in Marxist philosophy.[8] Young communist philosophers who might have wished to re-examine the matter were sternly reproved.[9]

Part of the French communist hostility to Hegel may be ascribed to the success of existentialist, neo-hegelian and Catholic appropriations of Hegel, which in the late 1940s and early 1950s were regarded by many commentators as antidotes to Marxism.[10] The postwar return to Hegel was therefore interpreted by many communists as a means by which the bourgeoisie, unable to sustain its previous positivist or neo-Kantian rejections of the dialectic, was now embracing the dialectic in

---

5 Cornu, *Karl Marx et la pensée moderne*, 1948.
6 Cornu, 'L'idée d'aliénation chez Hegel, Feuerbach et Karl Marx', 1948.
7 Joseph Stalin, *Dalectical and Historical Materialism*, New York, International Publishers, 1940, p.5. Quoted from the English translation of the chapter on philosophy, which is frequently published separately.
8 See Armand & Cornu, 'Critique et autocritique', 1949; Lefebvre, 'Autocritique: Contribution à l'effort d'éclaircissement idéologique', 1949.
9 See among others Lucien Sève, 'Hegel et le marxisme français', *La Pensée*, mars-avril 1988, pp.77-88.
10 See Weil, 'Hegel et son interprétation communiste', 1950.

its mystified Hegelian form in order to avoid conceding it in its revolutionary Marxist content.[11] The recurrent preoccupation of non-Marxists with the relation of Marx to Hegel appeared in this light as so many attempts to undermine the originality and intellectual force of Marx's mature work. The reduction of Marx to the Hegelian preoccupations of his youth would then be followed by a reduction of Hegel to the religious preoccupations of his own student days. But, by a negative dialectic that Hegel would have enjoyed, and not for the last time, the anti-Hegelian attacks mainly served to keep Hegel on the agenda.

After the death of Stalin, attitudes began to ease. The republication of Lenin's notes on reading Hegel, and the interest of George Lukács in Hegel and early Marx, were stimuli to reflexion. But so too was the extraordinary surge of interest in Hegel in all other areas of French intellectual life. Many intellectuals who had been attracted to communism by Henri Lefebvre's Hegelian Marxism, left the PCF in 1956 after the public revelation of Stalin's misdeeds and the Soviet intervention in Hungary. These included young people like Lucien Sebag, Pierre Fougeyrollas, François Châtelet and Edgar Morin,[12] who went on to develop their own radical post-Hegelian and post-Marxist conceptions.[13] Lefebvre himself returned to his exploration of Hegelian connections, though after his expulsion from the PCF in 1958 he accepted the logic of his view that Marx's critique of Hegel had effectively announced the end of philosophy, and concentrated his efforts on political and sociological theory.

Stalin's passing created a vacuum of authority within Marxism, and there were many claimants to fill it. Some intellectuals were attracted by Mao Tse-tung's reformulations of the dialectic, which drew heavily on Lenin's reading of Hegel, though in tone and intent it was uncomfortably close to the old *Short Course*.[14] Others were attracted to the Hegelianised Marxism of the Italian communists. Among them was Roger Garaudy, who for a dozen years after the Liberation was the PCF's philosophical spokesman. He developed a conception of Marxist humanism, not unlike Lefebvre's, on the basis of which he explored the possibilities of dialogue with Catholics and existentialists. Inevitably encountering the question of Hegel, Garaudy undertook a major study

---

[11] See Bottigelli, 'A propos du retour à Hegel', 1950; Commission de critique du cercle des philosophes communistes, 'Le retour à Hegel: dernier mot du révisionnisme universitaire', 1950.

[12] See Morin, *Autocritique*, 1959.

[13] See Sebag, *Marxisme et structuralisme*, 1964; Fougeyrollas, *Contradiction et totalité*, 1964; Châtelet, *Hegel*, 1968.

[14] See Mao Tse-tung, *Oeuvres choisies*, 1955.

of his philosophy.[15] Attempting to avoid presenting Hegel either as the father of existentialism or as a Marxist *avant la lettre*, Garaudy argued that Hegel was the philosopher of the French Revolution and the new bourgeois era it inaugurated. A philosophy adequate to the end of that era, and to the socialist revolution which brought it about, would need both to take Hegel to his logical conclusion and to transcend his thought. It was his view that Marxism offered such a philosophy.

At the same time as Garaudy was working on Hegel, communist intellectuals in several countries were taking advantage of the post-Stalin liberalisations to explore the same set of issues, revolving round the role of Hegel in the formation of Marx's thought. Many of these discussions appeared in French translations,[16] and the humanistic tone of many of them chimed well with Garaudy's work. Interest was also fuelled by the appearance of earlier Eastern European works which had fallen victim to Stalinist suppression, including Karl Korsch's *Marxism and Philosophy*, and especially George Lukács's *History and Class Consciousness*, a work from the early 1920s, suppressed throughout the Stalinist period, which seemed to anticipate many of the Hegelian themes emerging from debates on the early Marx. The rapid growth of non-communist forms of Marxism after 1956 drew heavily on these sources to construct a loosely organised 'New Left' intellectual circle nourished by former communists, Marxist social democrats, and members of the small Trotskyite movements, like the former surrealist Pierre Naville.[17] Many of Lefebvre's earlier works were republished during the 1960s, and he was influential in offering a coherent Hegelian-Marxist rationality, even though he was deeply critical of Hegel's theory of the state.[18] The problem he felt was that, having given a penetratingly accurate account of the state, Hegel then proceeded to justify its growing power.

The Sino-Soviet rift of the early 1960s was reflected in France in the emergence inside and outside the PCF of student groups which looked to China for leadership, and especially to the thoughts of Mao Tse-tung. Louis Althusser, a PCF member and also Secretary of the Ecole Normale, was not himself a 'Maoist' but developed some of Mao's philosophical positions as the basis for a new reformulation of dialectics. With it he hoped to lay the basis for a new political strategy for communism which would escape from the dead hand of Stalinism as well as from the humanistic versions of Marxism which he saw as thinly

---

[15] Garaudy, *Dieu est mort, étude sur Hegel*, 1962.
[16] See especially *Recherches internationales*, 1960.
[17] Naville, *Le nouveau Léviathan*, 1957; Rubel, *Karl Marx*, 1957.
[18] See Lefebvre, *Hegel, Marx, Nietzsche, ou le Royaume des ombres*, 1975; Lefebvre, *De l'Etat*, 1976-77.

disguised substitutes for Stalinism. His work was immediately influential among the politicised students of the mid-1960s and over time came to set the agenda for much Marxist debate worldwide.

Althusser sought to discount Marx's early writings as pre-Marxist, arguing that the mature Marx had established his great theoretical innovation by means of a radical rejection of the speculative philosophy of Hegel and Feuerbach. As a result of this revolution in theory, Althusser argued, Marx had made an epistemological break which enabled him to move on to the entirely new terrain of scientific thought, or theoretical practice, as opposed to the speculation, or ideological practice, which he left behind. However, since Marx had neglected to return to philosophy after this break, it still remained to make explicit the conceptual procedures which he had implicitly adopted as the basis for the new scientific approach, in other words to elaborate the theory of theoretical practice. Althusser therefore proposed to reformulate the Marxist dialectic in such a way that it would be purged of all the Hegelian mystifications which still clung to it. To this end, he introduced concepts drawn from Spinoza, Freud and Lacan to construct a theory of structural relations which would explain the social processes of domination and development in place of the Hegelian notions of expression, negation, mediation and sublation (Aufhebung).[19] The Marxist anthropologist Maurice Godelier was developing a comparable analysis at the same time.[20] He wished to purge the Hegelian residues so as to formulate an account of dialectics compatible both with data processing and structural anthropology. In his view the Hegelian notion of contradiction as the *identity* of opposites was irreconcilable with the Marxian notion of the *unity* of opposites.[21] One of the most incisive Marxist philosophers, Georges Labica, attempted to develop a more complex account of the discontinuities between Hegel and Marx.[22] He showed that the young Marx had made several attempts to think his way out of the Hegelian framework before finally leaving it, and leaving philosophy with it. Pierre Macherey, best known for his application of Althusser to literary theory, took up Althusser's use of Spinoza to argue that the latter was the only philosopher who offered the basis for a radical critique of Hegelian conceptions, and his book *Hegel ou Spinoza* (1979) attempted to elucidate the problem of developing a non-idealist dialectic. Other figures like Nicos Poulantzas, Etienne Balibar and Jacques Rancière contributed to the movement from differing political standpoints to construct a structural Marxism as a major alternative to Hegelianising Marxism during the 1960s and 1970s.

---

19 See Althusser *Pour Marx* (1965) and *Lénine et la philosophie* (1969).
20 See Godelier, 'Economie politique et philosophie', 1963.
21 See Godelier, *Horizons, trajets marxistes en anthropologie*, 1977.
22 Labica, *Le statut marxiste de la philosophie*, 1976.

The conflicts between Garaudy and Althusser and their followers produced some electrifying debates during the mid-1960s. Ironically, though, the aggressive anti-Hegelianism of the Althusserians served to provoke intensified study of Hegel and his relation to Marx, even among their own number. The events of May and June 1968 in France were the occasion for claim and counter-claim as to whose position had been vindicated by them. Garaudy, expelled from the PCF and newly converted to Catholicism, increasingly pursued a transcendental humanism which saw the Hegelian dialectic as a principle of hope, a notion he shared with the German philosopher Ernst Bloch.[23] But his defence of Hegel was taken up by numerous secular Marxists who considered Althusser was impoverishing Marxist theory. Lucien Sève's weighty treatise on human personality attempted to define a Marxist humanism which would avoid the excesses of Garaudy, but still retain the elements of the Hegelian dialectic which enabled Marxism to describe an intelligible relationship between the individual and society.[24]

The most prolific scholar of Hegel in France during the 1960s was also a Marxist, Jacques D'Hondt, whose major doctoral thesis in 1966 argued that Hegel's philosophy of history should be rehabilitated and subjected to a Marxist *dépassement*. This work was followed by half a dozen other books, both scholarly and popular, and by innumerable papers. D'Hondt argued for the unity of the early and late Hegel, and against the crude dismissal of his later activity as being that of a reactionary and self-seeking official philosopher of the Prussian state. He promoted study of Hegel's links with French thought, especially the nineteenth century socialists. And although his work was primarily historical, he vigorously defended the value of the Hegelian dialectic against the attacks of the Althusserians, whom he parodied as 'rupturalists'.[25] Without a Hegelian conception of the unity of opposites, he suggested, the key notion of contradiction collapses and there can be no adequate conception of development or process.

D'Hondt's work, together with that of Sève, provided a stimulus to many discussions in the 1970s which attempted to redefine an adequate philosophical basis for the new political directions taken by the world communist movement. Arcane debates over contradiction (how many types, how they could be resolved, conciliated or mediated, how they related to each other and to the process they were part of) used Hegelian terminology to think through, at one remove, the problems of political

---

[23] See Garaudy, *L'Alternative*, Paris, Robert Laffont, 1972.
[24] Sève, *Marxisme et théorie de la personnalité*, 1969.
[25] See D'Hondt, *L'Idéologie de la rupture*, 1978.

alliances of the French Left, Eurocommunism, relations with and between existing socialist countries, and issues of world peace.[26] Lucien Sève, following in Lefebvre's footsteps, assimilated an increasing number of reworked Hegelian concepts into his formulation of dialectics, culminating in his compendious work *Une introduction à la philosophie marxiste* (1980). The young Marxist philosopher Solange Mercier-Josa took a leaf out of Althusser's book to renew Marx by viewing him from a non-Marxist philosophical perspective. But instead of the perspective of Spinoza, she viewed him from the perspective of Hegel, arguing that this would allow her to generate new concepts which would enrich Marxist philosophy, retrieving even more than Marx did from the vast resources of the Hegelian system.[27]

Increasingly, during the 1970s, Marxist debates on Hegel in France became part of the wider international debates. This was partly reflected in the number of translations into French of the works of Lukács, Marcuse, Bloch, Horkheimer, Colletti, Badaloni, Schaff, Goulian, Oizerman and others. And it was also reflected in the debates at the growing numbers of international conferences, many of them reported in the French press.

However, a sea-change became apparent during the 1980s, whose consequences still remain to be seen. The declining fortunes of the French communist movement and the collapse of Marxist-Leninist and Trotskyite movements, combined with the withdrawal from them of large numbers of intellectuals, sharply reduced the constituency within which Hegel's role in Marxism was of political concern. The dramatic collapse of communism in Eastern Europe and the Soviet Union has accelerated the process. When in 1988 the PCF philosophical journal *La Pensée* asked 'Que faire avec Hegel?', the tone was set by Sève's retrospective essay, regretting the philosophical ravages of Stalinism, and by the calmly academic perspective of the other contributions. The Marxist intellectuals have largely reconciled their political affiliations with their professional careers, to the advantage of the latter. The explicit context of their writing is less often the *histoire événementielle* of day-to-day political and social struggle, and more often the *longue durée* of historical shifts in the pattern of civilisation. On such a view, the philosophical conflicts of the 19th century appear as recent family quarrels. Hegel and Marx then seem simply to offer competing answers to the same questions, while it is the questions themselves which need to be challenged, along with the unexamined assumptions of the intellectual history of Western Europe. How deeply this process of reappraisal will bite is as yet unclear, though it can confidently be predicted that the

---

26 See especially Etienne Balibar et al., *Sur la dialectique*, 1977.
27 Mercier-Josa, *Lire Marx et Hegel*, 1980.

fates of Hegel and Marx will be inextricably bound together in the process.

CHAPTER EIGHT
HEGEL AND CATHOLICISM

Proscribed by the religious authorities in the nineteenth century, Hegel was generally ignored by Catholics during the early part of the twentieth. When his name was mentioned at all, it was generally associated with totalitarianism in philosophy or in politics, and with the dangers of protestantism or, perhaps worse, of atheism. The rediscovery of Hegel's Christian dimension came primarily as a result of Jean Wahl's pioneering work in the decade before the Second World War. Wahl was familiar with the forms of protestant spirituality and mysticism which fed into Hegel's early thought, and his interpretation of the *Phenomenology* was strongly directed towards reaffirming its value as an account of spiritual experience. He even showed Hegel as sharing common concerns with Kierkegaard, who was popularly cast as the arch anti-Hegelian. Such a Hegel had some appeal for progressive Catholics like Paul Archambault and Gabriel Marcel, who were exploring new approaches to spirituality as part of a wider Catholic renewal, but for the most part they preferred to draw on more clearly existential sources for their inspiration. On the other hand, Wahl's work did draw Hegel to the attention of Thomist writers like Aimé Forest and Henri Rondet, who in due course came to respect the rational and systematic aspects of Hegel.

In parallel with Wahl, the Jesuit philosopher Gaston Fessard was also discovering Hegel during the late 1920s, though he was obliged to keep his writings private, and was forbidden by his Order to allow the *Revue philosophique* to print an article of his which had been planned for the Hegel centenary issue of 1931. He subsequently became a prominent member of Kojève's seminar, and presented one of the two concluding papers for it in 1939. Applying Hegelian logic to his Catholic faith, Fessard developed a dialectical account of St Ignatius Loyola's spiritual exercises, and as a teacher and an editor of the Jesuit journal *Etudes*, Fessard did a great deal to foster critical interest in Hegel among Catholic intellectuals throughout his long life.[1]

It was not until the Liberation that the fruits of Wahl's and Fessard's labours became apparent within the Catholic tradition, and Hegel's

---

[1] See Fessard, *Hegel, le christianisme et l'histoire*, 1990. Fessard died in 1978, aged 81.

'official' rehabilitation was secured by French Jesuit theologians. Father Henri Niel's thesis, *De la médiation dans la philosophie de Hegel* (1945) was the major breakthrough. The title was deceptively modest since the concept of mediation is virtually synonymous with the dialectic, which in turn is the core of Hegelian philosophy. What Niel proposed was a very substantial account of Hegel's entire philosophical endeavour. Although he considered Hegel was wrong to assert that all mediations could be transcended, he argued strongly that his philosophy was fundamentally theistic, and could form the basis of a rational metaphysics. This conclusion was contested by Kojève among others, but Niel responded that if Hegel had been an atheist, neither Feuerbach nor Marx would have been so anxious to criticise him.[2] Niel was supported in his view by Gaston Fessard, who felt that despite the atheistic conclusions drawn by his former tutor and by Marxist interpreters, an intelligent reading of Hegel could 'open the most magnificent path to restoring their full relevance to the historical and eternal truths of Christianity'.[3]

Whatever the disputes and ambiguities that followed, it is clear that in the immediate aftermath of the war, Hegel was suddenly and dramatically restored to the canon of secular philosophers acceptable for Catholics to read. On the one hand this provided a limited, but spectacular, rebirth for the old Right Hegelianism which had taken its mission to be one of theodicy, justifying the ways of God to Man. On the other it provided an 'opening to the Left' for Catholics, enabling dialogue to take place with the latter-day Left-Hegelians, in the guise of Marxists and existentialists.

Fessard was the most trenchant of the Right Hegelians. An able dialectician, he was vehemently opposed to the communists, and to a lesser extent the existentialists, seeing Hegel as a well-stocked armoury for his attacks on them. He also found there weapons with which to attack the Thomists, whose disregard for history left them, in his view, perilously vulnerable to Marxism, though he conceded that Hegel's own attitude to history had been characterised by a profound ambivalence.[4] Ultimately, though, debate was less about interpretations of Hegel than about the concrete issues which could be theorised in Hegelian or Marxist terms, especially the political stance of the Catholic Church in the face of issues such as its relations with Eastern European governments, its pastoral role in working class areas, or its part in the liberation struggles of the Third World.

---

[2] See Kojève, 'Hegel, Marx et le christianisme', 1946, and the response in Niel, 'L'interprétation de Hegel', 1947.

[3] Fessard, 'Deux interprètes de la Phénoménologie de Hegel', 1947, p.373.

[4] See Fessard, *De l'actualité historique*, 1960.

The Thomists, for their part, were not unduly abashed by Fessard's criticisms, and were inclined to respond that too slavish an adoption of Hegel's theory of history could leave a Christian trapped in its immanentism, unable to achieve the transcendent view which truly moral action required. They were, of course, thinking of Marxism and the danger that the Hegelian dialectic could all too easily lead to an unpalatable materialism, or an equally unacceptable revolutionary militancy. Their philosophical journal, *La Revue Thomiste*, kept assiduously abreast of the rising tide of Hegelianism with review essays and theological discussions, and the international conference of Thomists in Rome in 1955 devoted great attention to a comparison of Hegel and St Thomas Aquinas.[5] No doubt this effort was in part an attempt to restore Thomism's flagging vitality, but it also sprang from an awareness that the Kantian lens through which Aquinas had largely been viewed could in some cases be advantageously replaced by a Hegelian one.

The intense polarisations of the Cold War were responsible for much of the lingering coolness towards Hegel, behind whom Marx could be seen to lurk. The Thomist Dominican, Georges Cottier, saw Marxism as essentially a phase in the development of Hegelianism, whose atheism it inherited.[6] Henri Niel, on the other hand, maintained his belief in the value of Hegel for Catholicism, and was bolder than most of his fellows in broaching the Hegel-Marx relation. During the 1950s, he wrote extensively on the origins of Marxism in the Young Hegelian movement, the concept of work in Hegel and Marx, and the implications of Hegelian and Marxist ideas for a Christian view of history. After he had opened up these themes for Catholic philosophers he was followed by many others, working towards a dialogue with Marxism and using Hegel as mediator.

The problem of existentialism was almost as disturbing for Catholics, and the Liberation period saw many anathematisations of Sartre and his epigones. However, the political rapprochement between existentialists and Left-wing Catholic intellectuals on issues of war and peace, international relations and social and economic policy gave a practical context to the philosophical rapprochement between Catholic thought and existential neo-Hegelianism, from the late 1940s. Inspired in part by Jean Wahl's work, many Catholics came to view phenomenology as a resource rather than a threat for their faith. Theologians like Alphonse de Waelhens and Stanislas Breton explored Hegelian notions of identity, difference, contradiction and consciousness in their relation to similar notions in Husserl or Heidegger. In the process they did as much as any to cement the preeminence of the 'three H's' in postwar philosophy.

---

[5] *Sapienta Aquinatis. Communicationes IV. Congressus Thomistici internationalis. Romae, 13-17 Septembris 1955*, 1955.
[6] See Cottier, *L'Athéisme du jeune Marx*, 1959.

Catholic philosophers like Maurice de Gandillac and Mikel Dufrenne helped to confirm Hegel's value not only for a humanistic philosophy of consciousness but also for a Catholic conception of concrete human existence. But few went as far as *abbé* Paul Touilleux, who reformulated both Marx and Hegel in terms of Kojève's analysis of the Master-Slave relationship.[7]

During the 1950s, perhaps the most prolific source of Catholic reflection on Hegel in French was a group of theologians at the university of Louvain who, though situated in Belgium, were widely followed in France. Their leading figure, Franz Grégoire, saw Hegel as the major source of Marx's philosophy, even though Marx had followed Feuerbach in rejecting the religious implications of Hegel.[8] Though he was initially inclined to see Hegel as a pantheist, Grégoire developed a more nuanced view, arguing that he was not an atheist but that there could be no final certainty on what his religious views had really been. During the 1950s Grégoire wrote voluminously,[9] seeking to reverse the neglect into which the more systematic aspects of Hegel had fallen. The later works in particular had been regarded as rigid, lifeless and less amenable to Christian interpretations than the earlier more mystical and romantic works. Grégoire attempted to reveal the spiritual wealth of the later works, and especially to dispel the forbidding reputation of Hegel's theory of the state, from which he thought Christians could derive a more sophisticated understanding of politics.

His Louvain colleague, Paul Asveld, was closer to the dominant Catholic view in concentrating on the writings and activities of Hegel as a young man.[10] He presented the young Hegel as a would-be religious reformer, spurred on by a deep consciousness of spiritual alienation, which he saw permeating many aspects of modern experience. Hegel's conception of freedom was largely accepted by Marx, he agreed, but Hegel's method of analysis was one which could be used to good effect by Catholics, provided they took care to avoid sacrificing transcendence through excessive emphasis on the immanence of existence. Writing in 1960, Adrien Peperzak agreed that the young Hegel was the key to the mature system.[11] He felt, however, that Asveld's view was somewhat unilateral in over-emphasising the religious dimension at the expense of the political, and proposed to combine the two elements in a moral vision of the world.

---

[7] Touilleux, *Introduction aux systèmes de Marx et de Hegel*, 1960.

[8] Grégoire, *Aux sources de la pensée de Marx: Hegel, Feuerbach*, 1947.

[9] Many of his essays are collected in his *Etudes hégéliennes* (1958).

[10] Asveld, *La Pensée religieux du jeune Hegel, liberté et aliénation*, 1953.

[11] Peperzak, *Le jeune Hegel et la vision morale du monde*, 1960.

By the early 1960s, the abating of the Cold War and the wind of change within the Church opened the way for fundamental reappraisals of Catholic philosophy. The reforming papacy of John XXIII (1958-63) and the Second Vatican Council which he called (1962-4) encouraged fresh thinking. There was widespread agreement that some of the most intractable problems of doctrine were inherent in the narrowly Aristotelian conceptual framework which had traditionally been adopted to articulate faith, rather than inherent in Catholic faith itself. Many philosophers and theologians turned to Hegelian philosophy as an alternative framework. From the mid-1960s onwards there was a plethora of work by Catholic scholars analysing and adapting Hegel's major writings to reach new understandings of their own faith.

In France the agenda was set by theologians working at the Catholic Institute in Paris, who asserted the value of a Hegelian approach to religion. In two influential theses of 1964, Claude Bruaire developed the view that Hegel's work was an attempt to restate the Christian religion in philosophical language.[12] Its limitation was that God cannot be known or comprehensively conceptualised within language, however complex or subtle the linguistic apparatus. Hegel's construction of a logic of existence was therefore an affirmation of God, even if it failed to encompass God in thought. If the systematic pretensions were abandoned, along with the rather dogmatic view of Church history, Bruaire considered that theologians could fruitfully use Hegel's philosophy. His colleague Father Albert Chapelle shared the view that Hegel was a sincere believer who had sought to express his faith in philosophical terms. In a series of works on Hegel and religion he presented the Hegelian problematic as a rational hermeneutic of Christianity, which could provide the basic materials for a dialectical theology.[13]

Other Catholic commentators, including the Thomist Jesuit Henri Rondet, were arguing for a selective adoption of Hegel.[14] While agreeing that Hegel's own philosophical system contained unacceptable elements, related either to the pantheistic or protestant tendencies of his thought, they considered that the methodological value of his dialectic could be separated from these elements and set to work as a powerful tool for Catholic philosophy. This view had its analogies with the long-standing Marxist rejection of the idealist shell in favour of the dialectical kernel of Hegel, though it sometimes led to quite different results.

During the wave of concern over Hegel's own religious beliefs, much of the discussion focused on the early works with their more

---

12 Bruaire, *L'Affirmation de Dieu, essai sur la logique de l'existence*, 1964, and *Logique et religion chrétienne dans la philosophie de Hegel*, 1964.
13 Chapelle, *Hegel et la religion*, 3 vols, 1964, 1967 & 1971.
14 See Rondet, *Hégélianisme et christianisme*, 1965.

ostensibly religious preoccupations. Once this passed, attention moved to the later works, and despite some interest in the *Encyclopedia*,[15] it was primarily to the *Phenomenology of Mind* that Catholic philosophers looked for inspiration. Often it was read in a neo-existentialist perspective, as in François Guibal's analysis of the concept of God in the *Phenomenology*, drawing on Heideggerian and Lacanian approaches to elucidate the work's overall 'problematic', which could be applied to a series of theological and pastoral problems.[16] Similarly the Jesuit Father Conrad Boey found the conception of alienation in the *Phenomenology* provided a cogent alternative to the prevailing Marxist accounts.[17] Perhaps the most sustained work in this direction came from the Jesuit Father Pierre-Jean Labarrière. His doctoral thesis of 1968 was a close examination of the *Phenomenology*, carefully analysing its structures and dialectical movement, a theme to which he continually returned.[18]

However, Labarrière's major achievement was undoubtedly the scholarly translation of the *Science of Logic* which he produced with Gwendoline Jarczyck over a ten-year period (1972-81). Together and separately, Labarrière and Jarczyck have published many careful discussions on the details of Hegel's terminology and his logic,[19] taking Catholic interest in Hegel from the stage of assimilating Hegel's conclusions to that of learning to apply his method for themselves. The Dominican Dean of the Catholic Institute in Paris, Dominique Dubarle, was also influential in concentrating attention on Hegel's logic. He proposed a mathematical formalisation of the Hegelian dialectic as a basis for a new and richer logic.[20] The Louvain theologian André Léonard, author of a weighty thesis on Hegel's concept of faith, followed in 1974 with a paragraph by paragraph exegesis of the shorter *Logic from the Encyclopedia*.[21] Like Dubarle and Labarrière, he sought to throw light on the logical structuration of the Hegelian system in order to draw lessons for speculative theology.

These Hegelian explorations were of course not unique to French Catholic intellectuals. Catholic theologians from other countries contributed to stimulating their reflection, and some of the more notable

[15] See, for example, Quelquejeu, *La Volonté dans la philosophie de Hegel*, 1972. The Dominican writer focuses on the writings of 1821-31.
[16] Guibal, *Dieu selon Hegel*, 1975.
[17] Boey, *L'Aliénation dans la 'Phénoménologie de l'Esprit'*, 1970.
[18] See Labarrière, *Structures et mouvement dialectique dans la Phénoménologie de l'esprit*, 1968; and Labarrière, *La Phénoménologie de l'Esprit de Hegel: introduction à une lecture*, 1979.
[19] See Labarrière & Jarczyck, *Hegeliana*, 1986.
[20] Dubarle & Doz, *Logique et dialectique*, 1972.
[21] See Léonard, *Commentaire littéral de la 'Logique' de Hegel*, 1974; and Léonard, *La Foi chez Hegel*, 1970.

foreign works were translated into French. These included, among others, the writings of the German-Swiss Hans Küng, whose masterwork on the incarnation of God was translated in 1973. Küng proposed an introduction to Hegel's theology as the basis for a new Christology, or theology of God in the world. His work on Christology was continued by the Cuban Jesuit Emilio Brito, working in Louvain, who saw a purified Hegelianism as offering the foundations of a Christian vision of the Second Coming. Brito has recently commented that there are significant convergences between Hegel and St Thomas Aquinas on theological issues, though the growing impact of Hegel on Catholic thought has been accompanied by a declining interest in St Thomas.[22]

Undoubtedly Hegelian theology is still marked as 'advanced' and therefore risky in Catholic terms. But its legitimacy is very firmly established. Theologians who would not necessarily endorse its totalising aspirations nonetheless welcome the insights it offers in elucidating such traditional questions as the meaning of Evil, Sin or Freewill.[23] So, for example, Evil seen as finitude offers the hope of its being transcended by the infinite; Sin seen as an alienation makes a collective response possible; and Freedom seen as the knowledge of necessity enables human autonomy to be reconciled with divine omnipotence. No doubt human thought or language will always be held finally incapable of penetrating the mysteries of the deity and divine relations with the created universe. However, the subtle Hegelian dialectic apparently reaches parts that other theological approaches cannot reach, and in some respects Hegel has gained a position among 20th century French Catholic theologians analogous to his position among 19th century German Protestants.

Theology, and especially Christology, is a specialised and somewhat rarefied activity which seldom attracts widespread public notice. Perhaps more noticeable is Catholic social thought, where Hegel has also had a significant impact. It is a matter of some controversy among Catholics whether there is, or should be, a distinct Catholic social doctrine, especially if that is interpreted to confine discussion to the views expressed or implicit in papal encyclicals. Conservative thinking tends to favour the latter view, but within progressive circles there is a strong preference for adopting, and contributing to, secular social analyses. Most frequently they concentrate on conceptions produced within the socialist movement,

---

[22] Emilio Brito, 'La bonté de Dieu selon Thomas d'Aquin et Hegel', *Science et Esprit*, xxxix, octobre-décembre 1987, pp.281-300.
[23] See for example: Vergez, *Faute et liberté*, 1969; Boey, *L'Aliénation dans la 'Phénoménologie de l'Esprit'*, 1970; Quelquejeu, *La Volonté dans la philosophie de Hegel*, 1972; *Hegel et la théologie contemporaine: l'absolu dans l'histoire*, 1977; Jarczyk, *Système et liberté dans la Logique de Hegel*, 1980; Juszczak, *Hegel et la liberté*, 1980; Rosenfield, *Du mal: essai pour introduire en philosophie le concept du mal*, 1990.

where these can be separated from any atheistic implications. While Marxism has historically been the main source of progressive social theory, the role of Hegel was always acknowledged, and during the 1980s Hegel came to assume a more prominent position. In a work of 1984 subtitled 'How can one be a Christian after Marx and Hegel?', the pastoral theologian Hyppolite Simon argued that Hegel was in advance of Marx in arguing for greater autonomy of the state with respect to civil society.[24] Hegel's less reductive conception offered better prospects, in his view, for attributing more autonomy and value to the domains of philosophy, art and faith, dismissed by Marx as mere ideology. In the nature of their enterprise, however, progressive Catholics have usually declined to present their analysis of Hegel (or Marx) as a specifically Catholic social or political theory. The interventions of philosophers like Claude Bruaire, Joseph Gauvin or Jacques Taminiaux have formed part of the broader debates on Hegel's theory of the state, politics and religion, or conception of civil society.[25]

The prospects for Hegel replacing St Thomas or indeed Aristotle as the 'official' philosopher of the Catholic Church suffered a distinct setback with the election of the conservative Pope John Paul II. His strategy for reversing the progressive direction of Vatican II extended to curtailing innovations in theology, especially where distinctly protestant overtones could be detected. When Hans Küng had his theologian's licence revoked in 1985 there were echoes of the condemnation by the First Vatican Council of Hegelian theologian Anton Günther more than a century earlier. Nevertheless, philosophy, like nature, abhors a vacuum. Many philosophers acknowledge that traditional Catholic conceptions have demonstrated the limitations in their ability to understand the complex and changing character of the modern world. In consequence, Hegelian philosophy has become one of the strongest currents in contemporary Catholic thought, competing with and sometimes complementing Liberation Theology among Catholic intellectuals in France as elsewhere. However, Gaston Fessard remains a lone example of Right-Hegelianism, since in general the conservative wing of the Church has adopted anti-Hegelian positions rather than Right-Hegelian ones. With the declining influence of Marxism during the 1980s, Hegel has been felt by some Left Catholics to offer the conceptual advantages of Marxist theory without the latter's unattractive historical and political record. Paradoxical though it

---

[24] Simon, *Chrétiens dans l'état moderne ou Comment peut-on être chrétien après Marx et Hegel?*, 1984.

[25] See, for example, *Hegel-Jahrbuch 1967*, 1968, (Fessard & Bruaire); Gadamer, *Hegel-Tage Urbino 1965*, 1969, (Gauvin, Bruaire, Régnier, Tiliette); d'Hondt, *Hegel et Marx: la politique et le réel*, 1971 (Bruaire); Rosenfield, *Politique et liberté: une étude sur la structure logique de la 'Philosophie du droit' de Hegel*, 1984; Taminiaux, *Naissance de la philosophie hégélienne de l'état*, 1984; Planty-Bonjour, *Droit et liberté selon Hegel*, 1986.

may seem, the Catholic rediscovery of Hegel appears therefore to have rejuvenated not only Left-Catholicism but also Left-Hegelianism. And in the process it has created a forum and a common language within which Catholic and secular intellectuals can share their views.

CONCLUSION

Though the postwar history of Hegel in France is rich and plural, the three main currents of development have become increasingly intertwined and increasingly concentrated in the University, or rather universities, since they too are increasingly plural. In part this may be traced to the slow convergence of ideological networks, but in large measure it is undoubtedly a result of the wider professionalisation of French intellectual life.

For almost a century after the foundation of the Napoleonic University system, academic philosophy had a professional basis which was used to support a narrowly defined framework of ideas and values for the French state. The framework excluded or marginalised thought which overtly declared its allegiance either to organised religion and the political far Right or to the organised labour movement and the political far Left. In consequence, each of the excluded movements maintained its own counter-culture, with an ethos and distinct institutions to articulate its ideological directions. Towards the end of the 19th century the boundaries became more porous, first with the rise of energetic and respected socialist intellectuals, and later with the participation of Catholic intellectuals in university activity. Since the Second World War, and especially after the enormous expansion of higher education in the 1960s, the university system has become the predominant location within which different intellectual traditions contend. Conflicting currents may at times vie with one another for institutional power, and the conflicts of view may at times be sharply expressed, but they are increasingly seen as matters internal to a single intellectual community with agreed ground-rules and a more ecumenical approach to their differences. After all, the protagonists are frequently colleagues at the same or neighbouring establishments with no lack of practical concerns in common.

The attenuation of antagonism between competing currents of thought has created more space for the development of pluralistic and non-aligned philosophical enquiry. Most of the books appearing on Hegel observe the normal academic conventions of dispassionate analysis even where the approach is informed by an overarching personal conviction, declared or not. Many of them are minimally revised doctoral theses, which were appearing in print at a peak rate of three or four per year during the 1970's. To these may be added the large number of collective publications, often the result of a colloquium or the special number of a learned journal. No doubt the most distinguished of these was the volume published as *Hegel et la pensée moderne* in 1970, but it is not untypical of the genre. Originally a seminar series organised just before his death by Jean Hyppolite at the Collège de France, it included papers by Jacques Derrida, in the phenomenological tradition, by Jacques D'Hondt and Louis Althusser, from opposite wings of Marxism, by Dominique Dubarle and Marcel Regnier, from respectively the Dominican and Jesuit orders, and by Dominique Janicaud, a scholar best known for his study of Hegel and Ancient Greece. Each of the papers has its own specific interest, but together they encapsulate the main debates in which Hegel was being evoked in the late 1960s, and offer a spectrum of views rather than a unified partisan position.

Several intellectual centres have played a significant role in developing this pluralistic promotion of Hegel. The Centre for Research and Documentation on Hegel and Marx was founded by Jacques D'Hondt at the University of Poitiers in 1970. Apart from supporting a library and an information bulletin, the Centre has sponsored the translation of several minor Hegel texts, and published the proceedings of some nine colloquia.[1] An energetic Centre for Hegelian and Dialectical Studies with similar ambitions was set up in the early 1980s in Lausanne, in French-speaking Switzerland, under the directorship of Philippe Muller, whose own work, *Prévision et amour*, attempts to contruct a neo-Hegelian totalisation of European thought, encompassing philosophy, sociology, psychology and cultural theory among other things.[2] And a group based at the Ecole Normale at Saint-Cloud have published three substantial volumes of collective readings of the Science of Logic, as a result of a long series of seminars.[3] French academic philosophers have been regular participants in the conferences of the two or three international associations devoted to Hegel, and have generally kept a distance from the East-West political manoeuvring which has characterised the groupings. Conferences on Hegel have also been organised by philosophical associations and other academic institutions.

---

[1] The Centre's bulletin, *Recherches hégéliennes*, has appeared roughly twice yearly. Its published colloquia include *Hegel et Marx: la politique et le réel*, 1971; *Hegel et la pensée grecque*, 1974; *Hegel et le siècle des lumières*, 1974; *Hegel et la philosophie du droit*, 1979; *Science et dialectique chez Hegel et Marx*, 1980; *Phénoménologie hégélienne et husserlienne*, 1981; *Hegel et la religion*, 1982; *Phénoménologie et métqphysique*, 1984; *Droit et liberté selon Hegel*, 1986.
[2] The first two volumes of the projected three appeared in 1977 and 1985.
[3] Biard, editor, *Introduction à la lecture de la 'Science de la Logique' de Hegel*, 1981, 1983 & 1987.

Philosophical and literary journals have provided a regular forum for discussion of Hegel. Apart from the normal flow of scholarly work, many special numbers of journals have offered particular occasions for reflection on Hegel, whether or not from a particular thematic perspective. The bi-centenary of Hegel's death, 1970, produced a spate of such publications,[4] and so did the 150th anniversary, ten years later, of Hegel's birth.[5] These by no means exhaust even the special numbers on Hegel in learned journals, and in addition, French philosophers have been intermittent contributors to the two annual international journals devoted to Hegel, *Hegel-Jahrbuch* and *Hegel-Studien.*

It would be invidious to single out any of the scholarly monographs which have appeared in the last twenty years or so illuminating one aspect or another of Hegel's thought. A number of points of focus may be identified, however, centring on his *Logic*, especially the relation between rationality and freedom; on his political philosophy, especially the relation between the state and civil society; on his early work, especially during his period at Jena (1801-1805); and on the importance of Ancient Greece and its philosophers in his thought. In each of these four areas, several substantial studies have been produced which throw light on Hegel's thought and its importance in clarifying current philosophical problems.[6]

When Jean Hyppolite put Hegel on the agregation syllabus in 1950, this accession to France's senior competitive examination established Hegel's right to a place in French academic philosophy. There is no doubt that Hegel's place is now a central one. The study of his work has become a flourishing scholarly industry and his reputation has long ceased to depend on commentators with a particular political or ideological interest at heart. It seems probable that the extraordinary pitch of enthusiasm for Hegel in France began to recede in the mid-1980s, though it is early to judge. But even supposing a radical shift of fashion, the self-winding nature of academic activity will ensure a respectable continuation of Hegel studies for some time to come.

Ultimately though, whatever its aspirations to the condition of a self-developing concept, it is not the University machine that will settle the fate of Hegel. The University is steeped in French society, and

---

4 These included *Archives de philosophie, Revue internationale de philosophie, Revue de métaphysique et de morale, Revue de théologie et de philosophie,* and *Dialogue.*

5 These included *Archives de philosophie, Revue internationale de philosophie,* and *Revue de métaphysique et de morale.*

6 The particular works to which this analysis refers are listed in the bibliography, and in most cases the titles are self-explanatory.

increasingly caught in the tides of European and world history. Countervailing forces are at work changing the ideological configuration of France in ways which can as yet be only dimly perceived. The long decline of Catholicism and the collapse of communism offer both difficulties and opportunities to Hegelian ideas, as also do the rise of other forms of religion and the political realignments of the 1990s. The proliferating audiovisual media can offer enormous diffusion of ideas, but the 'sound bite' is the most Procrustean of beds for philosophical discourse. The Hegelian dialectic may offer a common language for a European intelligentsia brought together by economic as well as cultural bonds, but may well divide the same intellectuals from the plurality of other social and ethnic groups within their own societies. The global village is both more fragmented and more hegemonically totalised than before.

For more than fifty years, France has seen a major part of its prestige as lying in its assumption of the historic mantle of intellectual and cultural vanguard, shaping the ideas and values of Europe, the Western world, and even the world, *tout court*. Entering the last decade of the century every aspect of that role is now cast into question. Whether France can or should continue to claim intellectual leadership; whether it is still meaningful to speak of purely national cultures; whether the West, if it still exists, or even Europe, however conceived, can or should sustain a common intellectual culture; whether the mantle of history has passed, or is passing to somewhere else, East, West or South, if indeed history has not ended or at least abandoned mantles. The question is sharply posed as to whether Hegel and his legacy are part of the problem or part of the solution. But that is still in too many ways a new question. The twilight has not yet gathered and it is too early for Minerva's Owl to fly out in search of answers.

BIBLIOGRAPHY

SECTION ONE
FRENCH TRANSLATIONS OF HEGEL

There is no collected edition of Hegel's works translated into French. The following bibliography gives translations in the chronological order of their first publication. Where possible the most recent edition is also indicated. Unless otherwise shown, they are currently available in bookshops.

(1840-51)   *Cours d'esthétique*, tr. Charles Bénard, 3 vols, Paris, Joubert. Published in 1840, 1848 and 1851. No longer available.

(1854)   *La Logique subjective de Hégel*, tr. H. Sloman & J. Wallon, Paris, Ladrange, 139pp. No longer available.

(1855)   *Esthétique*, tr. Charles Bénard, untraced. 2nd edition published in 2 vols, Paris, G. Baillière, 1875, lxiv-496pp & 579pp. No longer available.

(1855)   *La Poétique*, tr. Charles Bénard, 2 vols, Paris, Ladrange. Extracted from (1855) *Esthétique*. No longer available.

(1859)   *Logique de Hegel*, tr. Augusto Véra, 2 vols, Paris, Ladrange. Second edition, containing additional material from the *Encyclopedia*, published by Baillière, 1874. Reprinted Bruxelles, 1969 in the collection 'Culture et civilisation', 880pp.

(1860)   *Système des beaux arts*, tr. Charles Bénard, Paris, Ladrange. Brief extract from (1855) *Esthétique*. No longer available.

(1863-66)   *Philosophie de la nature*, tr. Augusto Véra, 3 vols, Paris, Ladrange. Reprinted Bruxelles, 1969 in the collection 'Culture et civilisation'.

(1867-69)   *Philosophie de l'esprit*, tr. Augusto Véra, 2 vols, Paris, G. Baillière. Reprinted Bruxelles, 1969 in the collection 'Culture et civilisation', 996pp.

(1876-78)   *Philosophie de la religion*, tr. Augusto Véra, 2 vols, Paris, G. Baillière. Reprinted Bruxelles, 1969 in the collection 'Culture et civilisation', 922pp.

(1912)   Archambault, Paul, *Hegel: choix de textes et étude du système philosophique*, Paris, Michaud, 222pp, in the collection 'Les grands philosophes'. Reprinted in 1927, Paris, Rasmussen, No longer available.

(1928)   *La Vie de Jésus*, tr. D. D. Rosca, Paris, Gamber, 158pp. Reprinted Paris, Editions D'Aujourd'hui, 1976 in the collection 'Les introuvables'.

(1929)   "'Phänomenologie des Geistes" (p.158-166)', tr. Jean Wahl & Maurice Boucher, in Jean Wahl, *Le Malheur de la conscience dans la philosophie de Hegel*, Paris, Rieder, p.251-258. 2nd edition, Presses Universitaires de France, 1951, p.195-200. Now out of print.

(1937)   *Leçons sur la philosophie de l'histoire*, 2 vols, tr. Jean Gibelin, Paris, Vrin, 228pp & 242pp. With Prefaces by Edouard Gans and Karl Hegel. 2nd edition in 1 volume, 1945, 413pp. 4th edition 1987.

(1939)   *Morceaux choisis*, tr. Henri Lefebvre & Norbert Guterman, Paris, Gallimard. Reprinted in two volumes in the collection 'Idées', 1969, 313pp & 378pp.

(1939)   'Autonomie et dépendance de la conscience de soi; maîtrise et servitude', tr. Alexandre Kojève, with commentary, in *Mesures*, vol. 5, no. 1, 107-139. Reprinted in Kojève, *Introduction à la lecture de Hegel*, 1947, p.9-34.

(1939-41)   *La Phénoménologie de l'esprit*, tr. Jean Hyppolite, Paris, Aubier-Montaigne, in the collection 'Philosophie de l'Esprit', 2 volumes, 1939 & 1941, 368pp & 359pp. Reprinted subsequently by Aubier.

(1940)   *Principes de la philosophie du droit*, tr. André Kaan, Paris, Gallimard, 264pp. With an introduction by Jean Hyppolite. 7th edition 1949. Reprinted 1963, in the collection 'Idées', 382pp, and 1989 in the collection 'Tel'.

(1944)   *Esthétique*, 4 vols, tr. J. Gibelin & S. Jankélévitch, Paris, Aubier. No longer available.

(1947)   *Les Preuves de l'existence de Dieu*, tr. Henri Niel, Paris, Aubier, 248pp. No longer available.

(1947-49)   *Science de la logique*, 2 vols, tr. S. Jankélévitch, Paris, Aubier, 445pp & 581pp. Reprinted in four volumes, 1971. Currently out of print.

(1948)   Extracts in Klossowski, Pierre, *"Les Meditations bibliques" de Hamann. Avec une étude de Hegel*, Paris, Minuit.

(1948)   *L'Esprit du christianisme et son destin*, tr. Jacques Martin, with an introduction by Jean Hyppolite, Paris, Vrin, 176pp. 3rd edition 1971.

(1949)   'Extraits' in René Serreau & André Cresson, *Hegel, sa vie, son oeuvre*, Paris, Presses Universitaires de France, in the collection 'Philosophes', 152pp. Texts were translated by René Serreau. Reprinted 1961 & 1963, now out of print.

(1952)   *Précis de l'encyclopédie des sciences philosophiques*, tr. Jean Gibelin, Paris, Vrin, 320pp. 5th edition 1987.

(1952)   *Premières publications: Différence des systèmes philosophiques de Fichte et de Schelling; Foi et savoir*, tr. Marcel Méry, Paris, Vrin, 329pp. Reprinted in Gap by Editions Ophyrys, 1964 & 1970. No longer available.

(1954)   *Esthétique, Textes choisis par Claude Khodoss*, Paris, Presses Universitaires de France, 228pp. 12th edition 1988.

(1954)   *Leçons sur l'histoire de la philosophie*, tr. Jean Gibelin, Paris, Gallimard. Reprinted in 2 volumes, Paris, Gallimard, 1970 in the collection 'Idées'.

(1954-59)   *Leçons sur la philosophie de la religion*, 5 vols, tr. Jean Gibelin, Paris, Vrin. Reprinted 1970-72, 2nd edition 1975.

(1962-67)   *Correspondance*, 3 vols, tr. Jean Carrère, edited by Johannes Hoffmeister, Paris, Gallimard, 443pp, 379pp, and 437pp. Reprinted 1990 in the collection 'Tel'.

(1962)   *Hegel. Présentation, choix de textes, bibliographie*, ed. Kostas Papaioannou, Paris, Seghers, collection 'Philosophes de tous les temps', 207pp. Out of print.

(1963)   *Propédeutique philosophique*, tr. Maurice de Gandillac, Paris, Editions de Minuit, 239pp. Reprinted in 1964 by Gonthier in the collection 'Médiations'. Out of print.

(1964-65)   *Esthétique*, 8 vols (2 of which published in 2 parts each), tr. S. Jankélévitch, Paris, Aubier-Montaigne. Reprinted by Flammarion, 1979, in the collection 'Champ philosophique'.

(1964)   *Esthétique de la peinture figurative, textes réunis et présentés par Bernard Teyssedre*, Paris, Hermann, 187pp. Extracts from the Jankélévitch translation of *Esthétique*. Out of print.

(1965)   *La Raison dans l'histoire: Introduction à la philosophie de l'histoire*, tr. Kostas Papaioannou, Paris, Union générale d'éditions, collection '10/18', 313pp. Reprinted 1978.

(1966)   *Préface de la 'Phénoménologie de l'esprit'*, tr. Jean Hyppolite, Paris, Aubier-Montaigne, 224pp. A bilingual edition with the French and German texts on facing pages. 2nd edition 1978.

(1967)   'Extraits' in Jacques D'Hondt, *Hegel, sa vie, son oeuvre*, Paris, Presses Universitaires de France, collection 'Philosophes'.

(1969)   *La Première philosophie de l'esprit (Iéna 1803-4)*, tr. Guy Planty-Bonjour, Paris, Presses Universitaires de France, in the collection 'Epiméthée', 136pp.

(1970)   *Encyclopédie des sciences philosophiques en abrégé*, tr. Maurice de Gandillac, Paris, Gallimard, 552pp. Reprinted 1990.

(1970)   *Encyclopédie des sciences philosophiques, 1. Science de la logique*, tr. Bernard Bourgeois, Paris, Vrin, 646pp. 2nd edition 1979, reprinted 1986.

(1970)   *La Théorie de la mesure*, tr. André Doz, Paris, Presses Universitaires de France, in the collection 'Epiméthée'. A chapter from the *Science of Logic*.

(1970)   'Préface à la philosophie de la religion de D. Hinrichs', preceded by 'Lettres à Hinrichs', tr. Francis Guibal & Guy Petitdemange, *Archives de Philosophie* (Paris), vol. 33, 881-916. Not available commercially.

(1971-85)   *Leçons sur l'histoire de la philosophie*, 6 vols, tr. Pierre Garniron, Paris, Vrin, 1806pp.

(1972)   *Le Droit naturel*, tr. André Kaan, Paris, Gallimard, collection 'Idées', 186pp.

(1972)   *Des manières de traiter scientifiquement du droit naturel, de sa place dans la philosophie pratique et de son rapport aux sciences positives du droit*, tr. Bernard Bourgeois, Paris, Vrin, 104pp.

(1972)   *La Relation du scepticisme avec la philosophie, suivi de L'Essence de la critique philosophique*, tr. Bernard Fauquet, with a preface by Jean-Paul Dumont, Paris, Vrin, 99pp.

(1972-81)   *Science de la logique*, 3 vols, tr. Pierre-Jean Labarrière & Gwendoline Jarczyk, Aubier-Montaigne, 442pp, 336pp & 404pp.

(1974)   *La constitution de l'Allemagne 1800-1802*, tr. Michel Jacob, Paris, Editions Champ Libre. Out of print, but the text is included in *Ecrits politiques* (1977).

(1975)   *Principes de la philosophie du droit: ou droit naturel et science de l'état en abrégé*, tr. Robert Derathé & Jean-Paul Frick, Paris, Vrin, 376pp. 2nd edition 'revue et augmentée', 1982. 3rd edition 1989.

(1975)   *La Société civile bourgeoise*, tr. Jean-Pierre Lefebvre, Paris, Maspéro, in the collection 'Théorie: série textes', 143pp. No longer available.

(1975)   *Philosophie de l'histoire, textes choisis par Jacques D'Hondt*, Paris, Presses Universitaires de France, 151pp. Currently out of print.

(1976)   *Leçons sur Platon: 1825-1826*, tr. Jean-Louis Vieillard-Baron, Paris, Aubier, 167pp. Bilingual edition with French and German texts on facing pages.

(1976)   *Recension des oeuvres de F. H. Jacobi*, tr. par un groupe de travail sous la direction d'André Doz, Paris, Vrin, 56pp.

(1976)   *Système de la vie éthique*, tr. Jacques Taminiaux, Paris, Payot, 209pp.

(1977)   *Le Droit, la morale et la politique, textes choisis par Marie-Jeanne Königson*, Paris, Presses Universitaires de France, 192pp.

(1977)   *Ecrits politiques: La constitution de l'Allemagne, Actes de l'Assemblée des états du royaume de Wurtemberg, A propos du 'Reform Bill' anglais*, tr. Michel Jacob & Pierre Quillet, Paris, Editions Champ Libre, with a postface by Kostas Papaioannou, 424pp.

(1977)   *Le Savoir absolu*, tr. Bernard Rousset, Paris, Aubier Montaigne, 252pp. Bilingual edition of the last chapter of the *Phenomenology of Mind* with French and German texts on facing pages.

(1978)   *Textes pédagogiques*, tr. Bernard Bourgeois, Paris, Vrin, 162pp.

(1979)   *Les Orbites des planètes: dissertation de 1801*, tr. François de Gandt, Paris, Vrin, 203pp. With an introduction on Hegel's critique of Newtonian mechanics and a Preface by Dominique Dubarle.

Michael Kelly

(1980)	*Logique et métaphysique: Iéna 1804-1805*, tr. D. Souche-Dagues, Paris, Gallimard, with a commentary by André Kaan, 297pp.
(1981-82)	Collection 'Eleuthérologie', Paris, Alain Braik. A series of more than twenty short, unusually designed pamphlets in a variety of formats and colours, containing extracts from various of Hegel's works, either in German or French or both. No longer available.
(1981)	*Les Ecrits de Hamann*, tr. Jacques Colette, Paris, Aubier-Montaigne, 144pp.
(1982)	*La Philosophie de l'esprit: de la Realphilosophie 1805*, tr. Guy Planty-Bonjour, Paris, Presses Universitaires de France, 138pp.
(1984)	*La positivité de la religion chrétienne*, Paris, Presses Universitaires de France, collection 'Epiméthée', 144pp. A collective work, published under the direction of Guy Planty-Bonjour.
(1985)	*Introduction à la Science de la logique: Concept général de la logique*, tr. Fernand Cambon, Paris, Nathan, 1985, 103pp.
(1986)	*La différence entre les systèmes philosophiques de Fichte et de Schelling*, tr. Bernard Gilson, Paris, Vrin, 224pp. Edited with 'De la relation entre la philosophie de la nature et la philosophie en général', by Hegel or Schelling, and K. L. Reinhold, 'Eléments d'un tableau de la philosophie au début du XIXe siècle'.
(1986)	*La Météorologie*, tr. A. Véra, Paris, A. Braik, 1986, 38pp. An extract from the Véra translation of *Philosophie de la nature*, 1863-66.
(1987)	*Fragments de la période de Berne, 1793-1796*, tr. Robert Legros & Fabienne Verstraeten, Paris, Vrin, 112pp.
(1987)	*La Raison dans l'histoire*, ed. Jean-Paul Frick, Paris, Hatier, collection 'Profil philosophique', 78pp.
(1988)	*Encyclopédie des sciences philosophiques: 3, Philosophie de l'esprit*, tr. Bernard Bourgeois, Paris, Vrin, 608pp.
(1988)	*Foi et savoir: Kant, Jacobi, Fichte*, tr. Alexis Philonenko & Claude Lecouteux, Paris, Vrin, 208pp.
(1988)	*Journal d'un voyage dans les Alpes bernoises du 25 au 31 juillet 1796*, tr. Robert Legros & Fabienne Verstraeten, Paris, J. Millon, 113pp.
(1988)	*Qu'est-ce que la maladie?*, tr. A. Véra, Paris, A. Braik, 1988, 58pp. An extract from the Véra translation of *Philosophie de la nature*, 1863-66.
(1989)	*Comment le sens commun comprend la philosophie*, tr. Jean Lardic, Arles, Actes Sud, 128pp. With an essay 'La contingence chez Hegel'.
(1989)	*Hegel, le malheur de la conscience et l'accès à la raison*, Paris, Aubier, 161pp. Includes a bilingual edition of extracts from *La Phénoménologie de l'esprit*, translated by Gwendoline Jarczyk & Pierre-Jean Labarrière.

(1989)   *Le Syllogisme du pouvoir: y a-t-il une démocratie hégélienne?*,
Paris, Aubier, 362pp. Includes a bilingual edition of extracts from
La Philosophie du droit, translated by Gwendoline Jarczyk &
Pierre-Jean Labarrière.

SECTION TWO

PUBLICATIONS RELATING TO HEGEL IN FRENCH, 1826-1945

The list includes all works in French relating to Hegel published before 1945. It is ordered chronologically, books preceding articles within each year. References given in square brackets [ ] are the Bibliothèque Nationale library code.

1826

Cousin, Victor, *Fragmens philosophiques*, Paris, Ladrange, 1826. [Not in B.N.]. 2nd edition, revised with new Preface, Ladrange, 1833, lx-408pp, [R.32594].

1828

Cousin, Victor, *Cours de l'histoire de la philosophie*, 3 vols, Paris, Pichon & Didier, 1828-29, [R.32584-6]. The text of lectures given in the academic year 1828-29.
Cousin, Victor, *Cours de philosophie. Introduction à l'histoire de la philosophie*, Paris, Pichon & Didier, 1828. [R.32581]. The text of lectures given April-July 1828.
Lerminier, Eugène, 'De la nature du droit positif et de son importance nationale', *Le Globe*, tome vi, 28 juin 1828, p.505-506, [4° Z.3524 (6)].

1829

Lerminier, Eugène, *Introduction générale à l'histoire du droit*, Paris, A. Mesnier, 1829, xxv-445pp, [8° F.3760]. Chapter XVIII, 'Nouvelle école philosophique - M. Gans. Esquisse du système de M. Hegel', pp.259-271.

1831

Lerminier, Eugène, *Philosophie du droit*, 2 vols, Paris, Paulin, 1831, L-334pp & 463pp, [F.38712-3]. Especially vol. 2, Chapter IX, 'Schelling - Hegel', pp.189-218.
Quinet, Edgar, 'De la révolution et de la philosophie', *Revue des deux mondes*, iv, 1831, p.464-474.

1832

Lerminier, Eugène, *Lettres philosophiques adressées à un Berlinois,* Paris, Paulin, 1832, 412pp, [R.41667].
NN, 'Système de Hegel sur l'Etat', *Revue européenne*, no. xiii, 1832, p.73-88; no. xiv, 1832, p.219-232.

1834

Prévost, Amédée, 'Philosophie allemande, Hegel', *Revue du progrès social*, mai 1834, p.1-16; octobre 1834, p.16-45.

1835

Heine, Heinrich, *De l'Allemagne*, 2 vols, Paris, E. Renduel, 1835, published as *Œuvres*, vols 5 & 6, [Z.50378-9]. Volume 1, Chapter entitled 'De Kant jusqu'à Hegel', p.145-240. 2nd edition, Paris, Michel-Lévy, 1855, reproducing the same text p.115-184.

Lerminier, Eugène, *Au-delà du Rhin*, 2 vols, Paris, F.Bonnaire, 1835, 378pp & 364pp, [M.13802-3]. Volume 2, chapter entitled 'La philosophie allemande', p.109-149.

Schelling, F. W. J., 'Jugement de Schelling sur la philosophie de M. Cousin et sur l'état de la philosophie française et de la philosophie allemande en général', tr. J. Willm, *La Revue germanique*, 3e série, tome 4, octobre 1835, p.3-24. The Preface to a German translation of Cousin's *Fragments philosophiques*.

Willm, Joseph, 'Essai sur la philosophie de Hegel', *La Revue germanique*, 3e série, I, janvier 1835, p.22-37; II, avril 1835, p.119-133; III, juillet 1835, p.71-93; août 1835, p.177-209; V, mars 1836, p.251-266; IX, janvier 1837, p.1634; X, mai 1837, p.135-149; XI, septembre 1837, p.227-239; XII, novembre 1837, p.151-163; décembre 1837, p.239-258, [Z.58976-58989]. Published in volume form as *Essai sur la philosophie de Hegel*, Paris & Strasbourg, F.-G. Levrault, 1836, 102pp, [R.54067].

1836

Michelet, Karl-Ludwig, *Examen critique de l'ouvrage d'Aristote intitulé Métaphysique*, Paris, Mercklein, 1836, xl-322pp, [R.43840].

Penhoën, Barchou de, *Histoire de la Philosophie allemande depuis Leibnitz jusqu'à Hegel*, 2 vols, Paris, Charpentier, 1836, [R.27597-27598].

1838

Quinet, Edgar, 'De la vie de Jésus par le docteur Strauss', *Revue des deux mondes*, vol. 16, 1838, p.585-629.

1839

Cieszkowski, August de, *Du crédit et de la circulation*, Paris, Treuttel & Wurz, 1839, 315pp, [8°R.51641]. Reprinted, Paris, Guillaumin, 1847 and 1884.

Leroux, Pierre, *Réfutation de l'eclectisme*, Paris, C. Gosselin, 1839, xviii-348pp. Reprinted in his *Œuvres*, vols 1 & 2, Paris, Société typographique, 1850, [R.41686-41687].

Maret, *Essai sur le panthéisme dans les sociétés modernes*, Paris, 1839. 2nd edition 1841, xix-461pp.

Strauss, David Friedrich, *La vie de Jésus*, tr. E. Littré, 2 vols, Paris, Ladrange, 1839-40. 3rd edition 1864. Also a revised edition 1864.

1841

Gros, Dr, *De la personnalité de Dieu et de l'immortalité de l'âme, examen de quelques résultats de la philosophie allemande*, Berlin, chez Ascher & Paris, chez Brockhaus & Avenarius, 1841, vii-134pp, [R.37813].

Saintes, F. Armand, *Histoire critique du rationalisme en Allemagne depuis son origine jusqu'à nos jours*, Paris, J. Renouard, 1841, xi-456pp, [R.49995]. 2nd edition, Paris, Brockenhaus & Avenarius, 1843, [R.49996].

1842

Renouvier, Charles-Bernard-Joseph, *Manuel de philosophie moderne*, Paris, Paulin, 1842, xxxiii-446pp, [R.48840/m.21736].

Michael Kelly

Leroux, Pierre, 'Du cours de philosophie de Schelling. Aperçu de la situation de la philosophie en Allemagne', *La Revue indépendante*, tome III, mai 1842, p.289-348.

1843

Lèbre, A., 'Crise actuelle de la philosophie allemande: Ecole de Hegel, nouveau système de Schelling', *Revue des deux mondes*, tome i, 1 janvier 1843, p.5-42.
Taillandier, Saint-René, 'Situation intellectuelle de l'Allemagne. Vienne, Munich, Berlin', *Revue des deux mondes*, 1843, p.91-132.

1844

Cieszkowski, August von, *De la pairie et de l'aristocratie moderne*, Paris, Amyot, 1844, 164pp, [Lb 51.3915].
Ott, Auguste, *Hegel et la philosophie allemande*, Paris, Joubert, 1844, xii-544pp, [R.45527]. Subtitled 'exposé et examen critique des principaux systèmes de la philosophie allemande depuis Kant, et spécialement de celui de Hegel'.
Prévost, Louis, *Hégel, exposition de sa doctrine*, Paris, 1844, xxvi-331pp, [R.47509].
Taillandier, Saint-René, 'Un pamphlet du Dr Strauss (Julien l'Apostat)', *Revue des deux mondes*, 15 mai 1844, p.508-526.
Taillandier, Saint-René, 'De la littérature politique en Allemagne. 1. Les romanciers et les publicistes, la jeune Allemagne et la jeune école hégélienne', *Revue des deux mondes*, vol. 5, 1844, p.995-1040.
Taillandier, Saint-René, 'La poésie philosophique en Allemagne. Les poètes de la jeune école hégélienne: F. de Sallet et L. Schefer', *Revue des deux mondes*, 15 août 1844, p.582-600.

1845

Gans, Edouard, *L'histoire du droit de succession en France au moyen âge*, tr. L. de Loménie, Paris, Moquet, 1845, xxxi-239pp, [F.35326]. Preface, 'Quelques souvenirs sur M. Gans par M. Saint-Marc-Girardin', p.v-xxxi.
Rémusat, comte Charles-François-Marie de, *De la philosophie allemande*, Paris, Ladrange, 1845, clviii-208pp, [R.48651]. Subtitled 'Rapport à l'Académie des sciences morales et politiques, avec une introduction sur les doctrines de Kant, Fichte, Schelling et Hegel'.

1846

Proudhon, Pierre-Joseph, *Système des contradictions économiques, ou philosophie de la misère*, Paris, A. Lacroix, Verbeckhoven et Cie, 1846. Reprinted in his *Œuvres complètes*, Paris, 1850.
Willm, Joseph, *Histoire de la philosophie allemande depuis Kant jusqu'à Hegel*, 4 vols, Paris, Ladrange, 1846-49, [R.54068-54071]. Volume 3 (1849) is subtitled 'Hegel'.
Saisset, Emile-Edmond, 'La philosophie allemande; Des derniers travaux sur Kant, Fichte, Schelling et Hegel', *Revue des deux mondes*, tome xiii, 15 fevrier 1846, p.608-651.

1847

Taillandier, Saint-René, 'De la crise actuelle de la philosophie hégélienne: Les partis extrêmes en Allemagne', *Revue des deux mondes*, tome xix, 15 juillet 1847, p.238-268.
Willm, Joseph, 'Hegel', *Dictionnaire des sciences philosophiques*, edited by Adolphe Franck, vol. III, Paris, Hachette, 1847, p.26-43, [R.33707]. 2nd edition, Paris, Hachette, 1875, p.683-691.

1848

Taillandier, Saint-René, 'L'athéisme allemand et le socialisme français: Ch. Grun et Proudhon', *Revue des deux mondes*, 15 octobre 1848, p.280-322.

1849

Mickiewicz, Adam, *Les Slaves*, 5 vols, Paris, Au Comptoir des Imprimeurs Réunis, 1849, [Z.30469-73]. Subtitled 'cours professé au Collège de France (1840-44) et publié d'après les notes sténographiées'.

1850

Taillandier, Saint-René, 'La littérature en Allemagne depuis la Révolution de février. 1. La littérature politique, les philosophes et les poètes', *Revue des deux mondes*, 15 avril 1850, p.273-308.
Taillandier, Saint-René, 'La littérature en Allemagne depuis la Révolution de février. 2. L'histoire, le roman et le théâtre', *Revue des deux mondes*, 1 août 1850, p.465-505.

1852

Bénard, Charles-Magloire, *Hegel, philosophie de l'art, essai analytique et critique*, Paris, Ladrange & veuve Joubert, 1852, 315pp, [Z.Renan.1974].

1853

Cousin, Victor, *Du Vrai, du beau et du bien*, Paris, Didier, 1853, [R.32645]. Reprinted 1854, [R.32647].
Taillandier, Saint-René, 'Le mouvement littéraire de l'Allemagne. La rénovation philosophique et religieuse depuis 1850', *Revue des deux mondes*, 15 août 1853, p.633-662.

1854

Darboy, G., 'Théorie et pratique de la nouvelle philosophie allemande', *Le Correspondant*, 25 mai 1854, p.161-183.
Eckstein, Baron Gustave d', 'Essai d'une philosophie de l'histoire par le baron Barchou de Penhoën', *Le Correspondant*, 25 février 1854, p.671-708.

1855

Bartholmèss, Christian, *Histoire critique des doctrines religieuses de la philosophie moderne*, vol II, Paris, Ch. Meyrueis, 1855, [R.27738-27739].
Gratry, le père Alphonse-Joseph, *Philosophie: La Logique*, 2 vols, Paris, C. Douniol, 1855, [R.37707-37708]. Reprinted 6 times.
Véra, Augusto, *Introduction à la philosophie de Hegel*, Paris, A. Franck, 1855, 306pp, [8°R.70264]. Second edition published by Ladrange, 1864, 330pp, [R.53341], and reprinted Bruxelles in the collection 'Culture et civilisation', 1969.
Michelet, Charles, (Karl-Ludwig), 'De l'état actuel de la philosophie', *La Revue (philosophique et religieuse)*, 2, septembre 1855, p.129-143, [Z.23013].

1856

Dantier, A., 'La philosophie hégélienne et l'école populaire en Allemagne', *Revue contemporaine*, xxvi, 1856, p.682-717.

Fauvety, Charles, 'Logique subjective de Hegel, traduite par H.Sloman & J.Walon [sic]', *La Revue philosophique et religieuse*, mars 1856, p.487-9, [Z.23014].

Michelet, Charles, (Karl-Ludwig), 'Histoire critique des doctrines religieuses de la philosophie moderne par Christian Bartholmèss', *La Revue philosophique et religieuse*, mars 1856, p.369-393, [Z.23014].

Michelet, Charles, (Karl-Ludwig), 'Esquisse de logique', *La Revue philosophique et religieuse*, novembre 1856, p.385-413, [Z.23016]. Also published as a separate pamphlet Paris, Au bureau de la Revue, 1856, 29pp, [Rp.6076].

Saisset, Emile-Edmond, 'La philosophie moderne depuis Ramus jusqu'à Hegel', *Revue des deux mondes*, 1 mars 1856, p.5072.

1857

Cousin, Victor, *Fragments et souvenirs*, Paris, Didier, 1857, 535pp, [Z.46439]. Third edition 'considérablement augmentée'.

Cousin, Victor, 'Une promenade philosophique en Allemagne, Fragmens [sic] d'un journal de voyage, le début et l'épilogue', *Revue des deux mondes*, tome xi, 1857, p.535-560.

1858

Vacherot, Etienne, *La Métaphysique et la science ou principes de métaphysique positive*, 2 vols, Paris, Chamerot, 1858, [8°R.28867]. Vol. 2, Entretien 13, 'La philosophie du XIX siècle', p.322-489. Reprinted 1863.

Dolfuss, Charles, 'M. Cousin et l'Allemagne philosophique en 1817', *Revue germanique*, tome i, 1858, p.398-420.

Gasparin, comtesse A. E. (Valérie) de, 'L'Hégélien', in her book, *Les Horizons prochains*, Paris, Michel Lévy, 1858, p.111-136, [Y^2.42904]. Reprinted at least ten times.

Nefftzer, A., 'Hegel et la philosophie allemande', *Revue germanique*, vol. 3, ix, septembre 1858, p.574-594; vol. 4, xi, novembre 1858, p.388-411.

1859

Laugel, Auguste, Untitled review, *Revue des deux mondes*, 15 septembre 1859, p.511-512. Reviewing Véra's translation of Hegel's *Logic*.

Saisset, Emile-Edmond, *Essais de philosophie religieuse*, Paris, 1859, [8°R.56486]. Reprinted in 1862. Contains a chapter on 'Le panthéisme de Hegel', p.287-323.

1860

Janet, Paul-Alexandre-René, *Etudes sur la dialectique dans Platon et dans Hegel*, Paris, Ladrange, 1860, 397pp, [R.39288]. (The edition bears the imprint 1861, but is stamped 1860).

Saisset, Emile-Edmond, 'Leibnitz et Hegel, d'après de nouveaux documens [sic]', *Revue des deux mondes*, 15 décembre 1860, p.961-997.

1861

Levêque, Charles, *La Science du beau*, 2 vols, Paris, A. Durand, 1861. Volume 2 contains a chapter on 'Théorie de Hegel', p.539-555. 2nd edition 'revue et augmentée', 1872, [R.41861-2].

Véra, Augusto, *L'Hégélianisme et la philosophie*, Paris, Ladrange, 1861, 226pp. Reprinted Bruxelles in the collection 'Culture et civilisation', 1969.

Scherer, Edmond, 'Hegel et l'hégélianisme', *Revue des deux mondes*, 15 février 1861, p.812-856. Reprinted in his *Mélanges d'histoire religieuse*, Paris, Michel Lévy, 1864, 2nd edition 1865.

1862

Foucher de Careil, comte Alexandre Louis, *Hegel et Schopenhauer*, Paris, Hachette, 1862, xxxix-390pp, [R.36265]. Subtitled 'Etudes sur la philosophie allemande contemporaine depuis Kant jusqu'à nos jours'.

Saisset, Emile-Edmond, *Précurseurs et disciples de Descartes*, 2nd edition, Paris, Didier, 1862. Contains a chapter, 'Leibniz et la dernière philosophie allemande', p.401-466.

Véra, Augusto, *Mélanges philosophiques*, Paris, Vrin, 1862, 304pp. Contains an essay on 'La philosophie de la religion de Hegel'. Reprinted Bruxelles in the collection 'Culture et civilisation', 1969.

1864

Caro, Elme-Marie, *L'Idée de Dieu et ses nouveaux critiques*, Paris, Hachette, 1864, 508pp, [R.30639]. 4th edition, 1868.

Feuerbach, Ludwig, *Essence du christianisme*, tr. Joseph Roy, Paris, Lacroix, Verboeckhoven, 1864, 390pp.

Véra, Augusto, *Essais de philosophie hégélienne*, Paris, G. Baillière, 1864, 203pp, [R.53339]. The three essays are 'La peine de mort', 'Amour et philosophie', and 'Introduction à la philosophie de l'histoire'. Reprinted Bruxelles in the collection 'Culture et civilisation', 1969.

1865

Beaussire, Emile-Jacques-Armand, *Antécédents de l'Hégélianisme dans la philosophie française*, Paris, Germer-Baillière, 1865, xvi-236pp, [R.27954]. Subtitled 'Dom Deschamps, son système et son école d'après un manuscrit et des correspondances inédites du XVIIIe siècle.

Cousin, Victor, *Fragments philosophiques pour servir à l'histoire de la philosophie*, 5 vols, Paris, Didier, 1865-1866, [R.32602-32606].

Janet, Paul-Alexandre-René, 'Un précurseur français de Hegel, Dom Deschamps', *Revue des deux mondes*, vol. 58, 1865, p.244-251.

1866

Weber, Alfred, *Introduction historique à la philosophie hégélienne*, Strasbourg & Paris, Treuttel et Wurz, 1866, 20pp, [R.53900].

Cousin, Victor, 'Une promenade philosophique en Allemagne', *Revue des deux mondes*, vol 64, 1866, p.594-619.

Janet, Paul-Alexandre-René, 'L'histoire de la philosophie et l'éclecticisme', *Revue des deux mondes*, 15 janvier 1866, p.504-528.

1867

Mariano, Raphaël (Raffaele), *La Philosophie contemporaine en Italie, essais de philosophie hégélienne*, Paris, Baillière, 1867, 162pp, [R.43094].

Margerie, A. de, 'V. Cousin et son école', *Le Correspondant*, 25 juin 1867, p.424-461.

1868

Nourrisson, Jean-Félix, *Tableau des progrès de la pensée humaine depuis Thalès jusqu'à Hegel*, 3rd edition, Paris, Didier, 1868, R.45018]. The first edition, published in 1858, was 'jusqu'à Leibniz'. 6th edition, 1886.

Renouvier, Charles, 'De la philosophie du dix-neuvième siècle en France', *L'Année philosophique - Première année (1867)*, Paris, 1868, p.1-108.

Michael Kelly

Michelet, K.-L., 'L'hégélianisme en 1867', *Théologie et philosophie*, Geneva, 1868, p.130-143, [8°D.13314].

1869

Ferri, Luigi, *Essai sur l'histoire de la philosophie en Italie au XIXe siècle*, vol. 2, Paris, Durand, 1869.
Marrast, Augustin, *La Philosophie du droit de Hegel, essai analytique*, Paris, E. Maillet, 1869, 144pp, [R.43166].

1870

Taine, Hyppolite and Ernest Renan, Untitled article, *Journal des Débats*, 25 janvier 1870, p.3.

1871

Beaussire, Emile, 'Le centenaire de Hegel en 1870', *Revue des deux mondes*, 1 janvier 1871, p.145-161.
Beaussire, Emile, 'La philosophie politique de Hegel, à l'occasion de son centenaire', *Comptes rendus de l'Académie des sciences morales et politiques*, tome xxv, 1871, p.201-242.
Weber, Alfred, *Histoire de la philosophie européenne*, Paris, Fischbacher, 1871, [8°R.74498]. Reprinted several times 1883-1905.

1872

Renouvier, Charles, 'La doctrine hégélienne et la politique prussienne', *Critique philosophique*, 27 juin 1872, p.321-329.

1876

Bertauld, Pierre-Auguste, *De la méthode. Introduction à la recherche des causes premières*, vol. 1, Paris, Germer-Baillière & F. Alcan, 1876, [8°R.852 (I-IV)]. 2nd edition, 1891.

1877

Zeller, Eduard, *La Philosophie des Grecs*, tr. E. Boutroux, Paris, 1877.
Boutroux, E., 'E. Zeller et l'histoire de la philosophie', *Revue philosophique de la France et de l'étranger*, 2, vol 4, 1877, p.1-16, p.134-166, [8°R.847].

1878

Flint, Robert, *La Philosophie de l'histoire en France et Allemagne*, tr. L. Carrau, 2 vols, Paris, Baillère, 1878.

1880

Engels, Friedrich, *Socialisme utopique et socialisme scientifique*, tr. Paul Lafargue, Paris, Derveaux, 1880, 'Bibliothèque de la Revue socialiste', 1, 35pp.
Stahl, Frédéric-Jules, *Histoire de la Philosophie du Droit*, tr. A. Chauffard, Paris, E. Thorin, 1880, lxxvi-540pp, [8°F.1334].
Dieterich, K., 'David Friedrich Strauss et l'idéalisme allemand', *Revue philosophique de la France et de l'étranger*, 11, 1886, p.21-72.

1887

Funck-Brentano, Th., *Les sophistes allemands et les nihilistes russes*, Paris, Plon, 1887, [8°M.5241].

Auerbach, S., 'Georges-Guillaume-Frédéric Hegel', *Dictionnaire de pédagogie et d'instruction primaire*, vol. 1, Paris, Hachette, 1887, p.1242.

Valbert, G., 'La correspondance de Hegel', *Revue des deux mondes*, 1 juillet 1887, p.213-225. Reprinted in his *Profils étrangers*, Paris, Hachette, 1889, 2nd edition.

1889

Levy-Bruhl, Lucien, *La Théorie de l'état dans Hegel*, Paris, A. Picard, 1889, 20pp [8°R.Pièce.4331]. Extracted from *Comptes-rendus de l'Académie de sciences morales et politiques*, n.s. 32, vol. 49, 2e semestre, p.16-36.

1890

Levy-Bruhl, Lucien, *L'Allemagne depuis Leibniz, essai sur la conscience nationale en Allemagne, 1700-1848*, Paris, Hachette, 1890, iv-491pp, [8°M.6621, m7344].

1891

Jaurès, Jean-Léon, *De primis socialismi germanici lineamentis apud Lutherum, Kant, Fichte et Hegel*, Toulouse, A. Chauvin, 1891, [8°R.10563]. Published in French as *Les origines du socialisme allemand*, tr. A. Veber, Paris, Ecrivains Réunis, 1892, 93pp. The French version reprinted Paris, Ecrivains Réunis, 1928, and Paris, Maspéro, 1959.

1893

Delbos, Victor, *Le problème moral dans Spinoza et dans l'histoire du Spinozisme*, Paris, Alcan, 1893, [8°R.11759]. Chapter on Hegel, p.436-483.

Herr, Lucien, 'Hegel', in *La Grande Encyclopédie*, tome xix, Paris, Lamiraux, 1893-4, p.997-1003. Reprinted in L. Herr, *Choix d'écrits*, vol. 2, Paris, Rieder, 1932.

Lafargue, Paul, *L'Idéalisme et le matérialisme dans l'histoire*, Lille, G.Delory, 1893, 24pp. Also Paris, Henri Oriol, 'Bibliothèque socialiste', n.d., [Renan Z.8227], for which the date 1884 is given in the B.N. catalogue, without any apparent justification.

MacTaggart, J. Ellis, 'Du vrai sens de la dialectique de Hegel', *Revue de métaphysique et de morale*, novembre 1893, p.538-552, [8°R.12631].

1894

Amant, B., (pseud. Maurice Blondel), 'Une des sources de la pensée moderne: l'évolution du Spinozisme', *Annales de la philosophie chrétienne*, vol. 128, 1894, p.260-275, p.324-341.

Barrès, Maurice, *De Hegel aux cantines du Nord*, Paris, E. Sansot, 1894, 95pp. Reprinted 1904, [8°R.21246].

Noël Georges, 'La logique de Hegel', *Revue de métaphysique et de morale*, ii, 1894, 1, p.36-57; 2, p.270-298; 6, p.644-675; iii, 1895, 2, p.184-210; 5, p.503-526; iv, 1896, 1, p.62-85; 5, p.585-614. Reprinted as *La Logique de Hegel*, Paris, Alcan, 1897, 188pp, [8°R.14326]. Reprinted Paris, Vrin, 1933, 1938 and 1967.

Plekhanow, G., 'La philosophie de Hegel', *L'Ere nouvelle*, octobre 1894, p.138-146; novembre 1894, p.258-280, [8°Z.13759].

1895

Barthélémy-Saint-Hilaire, Jules, *Victor Cousin, sa vie et sa correspondance*, 3 vols, Paris, Hachette, 1895.

Jaurès, Jean, and Paul Lafargue, *L'Idéalisme et le matérialisme dans la conception de l'histoire*, Paris, Publications du Groupe des Etudiants Collectivistes, février 1895, 35pp, [8°R.Pièce 6048]. Subtitled 'Conférence de Jean Jaurès et réponse de Paul Lafargue'. Lafargue's text reprinted in *Cahiers du communisme*, septembre 1945, p.18-24.

Levy-Bruhl, Lucien, 'La crise de la métaphysique en Allemagne', *Revue des deux mondes*, 15 mai 1895, p.341-367.

Marx, Karl, 'Critique de la philosophie du droit de Hegel', tr. Ed. Fortin, *Devenir social*, septembre 1895. Reprinted at the same time as a separate piece by Giard and Brière, 15pp, [8°R.13595].

1896

Charléty, Sebastien, *Histoire du saint-simonisme (1825-1864)*, Paris, Hachette, 1896, 486pp.

Michel, Henry, *L'Idée de l'état*, Paris, Hachette, 1896, [8°R.13219]. Subtitled 'essai critique sur l'histoire des théories sociales et politiques en France depuis la Révolution'.

1897

Labriola, Antonio, *Essai sur la conception matérialiste de l'histoire*, Paris, Giard et Brière, 1897, 'Bibliothèque socialiste internationale'. With an introduction by Georges Sorel. Reprinted 1902, 1928, 1970.

Andler, Charles, *Les origines du socialisme d'Etat en Allemagne*, Paris, Alcan, 1897, 425pp, [8°M.9852]. 2nd edition, 1910.

Andler, Charles, 'La conception materialiste de l'histoire d'après M. Antonio Labriola', *Revue de métaphysique et de morale*, septembre 1897, p.644-658.

1898

Sombart, Werner, *Le Socialisme et le mouvement social au XIXe siècle*, Paris, Giard & Brière, 1898, [8°R.15180].

1900

Denis, abbé Charles, 'De l'influence de la philosophie de Kant et de celle de Hegel sur la critique historique appliquée aux origines chrétiennes', *Annales de philosophie chrétienne*, octobre 1900, p.95-106, [R.10292].

1901

Cornélissen, Christian, 'La dialectique dans l'oeuvre de Marx', *La Revue socialiste*, février 1901, p.185-200, [8°R.7135, m.408 (1-3)].

1902

Basch, Victor Guillaume, *La Poétique de Schiller*, Paris, Alcan, 1902. 2nd edition, 1911.

1903

Rappoport, Charles, *La philosophie de l'histoire, comme science de l'évolution*, Paris, Jacques, 1903, 'Bibliothèque d'études socialistes, 12', xv-247pp. Based on articles published in *La Revue socialiste*, 1900-1901.

1904

Basch, Victor Guillaume, *L'Individualisme anarchiste, Max Stirner*, Paris, Alcan, 1904, vi-294pp.

Croce, Benedetto, *L'Esthétique comme science de l'expression et linguistique générale*, tr. H. Bigot, 2 vols, Paris, Giard et Brière, 1904, 518pp.

Lévy, Albert, *La Philosophie de Feuerbach et son influence sur la littérature allemande*, Paris, Alcan, 1904, xxviii-545pp, [8°R.19264].

Grégoire de Tours, Frère, 'Hegel et saint Bonaventure', *Etudes franciscaines*, août 1904, p.143-148, [8°Z.15173].

1906

Stapfer, Paul, *Questions esthétiques et religieuses*, Paris, Alcan, 1906, 208pp.

Berth, E., 'B. Croce, "Ciò che è vivo e ciò che è morto della filosofia di Hegel"', *Revue générale de critique et bibliographie*, 4, no. 41, 1906, p.455-461.

1907

Leseine, Léopold, *L'Influence de Hegel sur Marx*, Paris, Bonvalot-Jouve, 1907, 257pp, [8°F.19524].

Berthelot, René, 'Thèse: Sur la nécessité, la finalité et la liberté chez Hegel', Bulletin de la Société française de philosophie, avril 1907, p.115-140. The transcript of a discussion of the thesis is given on pages 140-184. Berthelot's text is reprinted in his *Evolutionnisme et platonisme*, Paris, Alcan, 1908.

Jankélévitch, Serge, 'B. Croce, "Ciò che è vivo e ciò che è morto della filosofia di Hegel"', *Revue de synthèse historique*, vol 14, no. 41, 1907, p.235-239, [m.699].

1910

Croce, Benedetto, *Ce qui est vivant et ce qui est mort dans la philosophie de Hegel*, tr. Henri Buriot, Paris, Giard & Brière, 1910, xx-251pp, [8°R.23564]. Subtitled 'Essai critique suivi d'un essai de bibliographie hégélienne'.

Lévy, Albert, *David-Frédéric Strauss, la vie et l'oeuvre*, Paris, Alcan, 1910, iii-295pp, [8°M.14949].

Enriques, F., 'La Métaphysique de Hegel considérée d'un point de vue scientifique', *Revue de métaphysique et de morale*, xviii, no. 1, 1910, p.1-24.

Sorel, Georges, 'Vues sur les problèmes de la philosophie', *Revue de métaphysique et de morale*, 1910.

1911

Engels, Friedrich, *Philosophie, économie politique, socialisme, contre Eugène Dühring*, Paris, Giard & Brière, 1911, cxiv-420pp.

Hamelin, Octave, *Le Système de Descartes*, Paris, Alcan, 1911, xiv-392pp.

1912

Andler, Charles, editor, *La Philosophie allemande au XIXe siècle*, Paris, Alcan, 1912, vi-254pp. Contains an essay on Hegel by Victor Basch.

Roques, Paul-Etienne-Antoine, *Hegel, sa vie et ses oeuvres*, Paris, Alcan, 1912, 358pp, [8°M.16120].

Coutan, E., 'Note sur l'absolu et Dieu à propos de la philosophie hégélienne', *Annales de philosophie chrétienne*, vol 165, no.3, 1912, p.272-286, [R.10292].

1918

Duguit, Léon, 'Jean-Jacques Rousseau, Kant et Hegel', *Revue du droit public et de la science politique en France et à l'étranger*, xxiv, vol 35, 1918, avril-juin, p.173-211; juillet-septembre, p.325-377, [8°F.8814].

1919

Delbos, Victor, 'Les facteurs kantiens dans la philosophie allemande à la fin du XVIIIe siècle et au commencement du XIXe', *Revue de métaphysique et de morale*, 26, 1919, p.569-593; 27, 1920, p.1-25; 28, 1921, p.27-47; 29, 1922, p.157-176.

1920

Wahl, Jean, *Les Philosophes pluralistes d'Angleterre et d'Amérique*, Paris, Alcan, 1920, ii-312pp, [8°R.31503].

1921

Bréhier, Emile, *Histoire de la philosophie allemande*, Paris, Payot, 1921, 158pp, [8°Z.21054 (13)].
Meyerson, Emile, *De l'explication dans les sciences*, 2 vols, Paris, Payot, 1921, 368pp & 469pp, [8°R.33962].

1922

Papini, Georges, *Le Crépuscule des philosophes: Kant, Hegel, Comte, Spencer, Nietzsche*, Paris, E. Chiron, 1922, [8°R.31104].
Reynaud, L., *L'Influence allemande en France au XVIII et au XIX siècle*, Paris, 1922.

1923

Groethuysen, Bernard, 'Les Jeunes Hégéliens et les origines du socialisme contemporain en Allemagne', *Revue philosophique de la France et de l'étranger*, 95, mai-juin 1923, p.379-402.
Valensin, Auguste, 'Histoire de la philosophie d'après Hegel', *Archives de la philosophie*, 1, no. 1, 1923-34, p.81-91. Reprinted in his book *A travers la métaphysique*, Paris, G. Beauchesne, 1925, 251pp, [8°R.34095].

1924

Groethuysen, Bernard, 'La Conception de l'état de Hegel et la philosophie politique en Allemagne', *Revue philosophique de la France et de l'étranger*, 97, mars-avril 1924, p.180-207.

1926

Boutroux, Emile, *Etudes d'histoire de la philosophie allemande*, Paris, Vrin, 1926, 257pp.
Wahl, Jean, 'Note sur la démarche de la pensée de Hegel', *Revue philosophique de la France et de l'étranger*, 51, 1926, p.281-289. Reprinted in his *Malheur de la conscience*, 1929.

1927

Archambault, Paul, *Hegel: Choix de textes et étude du système philosophique*, Paris, Vald. Rasmussen, 1927, 222p, collection 'Les Grands philosophes français et étrangers', [8°R.22846 (4)].

Basch, Victor, *Les Doctrines politiques des philosophes classiques de l'Allemagne: Leibnitz, Kant, Fichte, Hegel*, Paris, Alcan, 1927, ix-366pp, [8°R.35660].

Brunschvicg, Léon, *Le Progrès de la conscience dans la philosophie occidentale*, vol. 1, Paris, Félix Alcan, 1927, [8°R.36328].

Eggli, E., *Schiller et le romantisme français*, 2 vols, Paris, Gamber, 1927. The index was published in 1928.

Marx, Karl & Friedrich Engels, *Œuvres philosophiques*, tr. J. Molitor, vols 1 & 2, Paris, Editions Coste, 1927.

Plekhanov, G. V. *Questions fondamentales du marxisme*, Paris, Imprimerie Centrale, 1927, 128pp.

Metz, A., 'Philosophie de la nature de Hegel', *Mercure de France*, année 38, vol. 198, 1927, p.61-69.

Sée, Henri, 'Remarques sur la philosophie de l'histoire de Hegel', *Revue d'Histoire de la Philosophie*, juillet-septembre 1927, p.321-334, [8°R.35149].

Wahl, Jean, 'Commentaire d'un passage de la "Phénoménologie de l'esprit" de Hegel', *Revue de métaphysique et de morale*, 34, no. 4, 1927, p.441-471. Reprinted in his *Malheur de la conscience*, 1929.

Wahl, Jean, 'La place de l'idée du malheur de la conscience dans la formation des théories de Hegel', *Revue philosophique de la France et de l'étranger*, 52, no. 9/10, 1927, p.103-147. Reprinted in his *Malheur de la conscience*, 1929.

Wahl, Jean, 'Sur la formation de la théorie hégélienne du Begriff', *Revue d'Histoire de la Philosophie*, octobre-décembre 1927, p.437-456; janvier-mars 1928, p.72-92, [8°R.35149]. Reprinted in his *Malheur de la conscience*, 1929.

1928

Rosca, D. D., *L'Influence de Hegel sur Taine, théoricien de la connaissance et de l'art*, Paris, Gamber, 1928, 432pp, [8°R.36486].

1929

Wahl, Jean, *Le Malheur de la conscience dans la philosophie de Hegel*, Paris, Rieder, 1929, 264pp, collection 'Philosophie', [8°R.32146 (5)]. Reprinted by Presses Universitaires de France, Paris, 1951.

Marcel, Gabriel, 'Le malheur de la conscience dans la philosophie de Hegel', *Europe*, 81, 15 septembre 1929, p.149-152, [8°Z.22011].

Tchijéwsky, D., 'Hegel et Nietzsche', *Revue d'Histoire de la Philosophie*, juillet-septembre 1929, p.321-347.

1930

Tronchon, Henri, *Romantisme et pré-romantisme*, Paris, Les Belles Lettres, 1930, viii-300pp, [8°Z.23542 (6)].

Zaleski, Z. L., *Mélanges d'histoire littéraire générale et comparée*, vol. 1, Paris, Champion, 1930. Contains a section on 'Edgar Quinet et Auguste Cieszkowski'.

1931

Forest, Aimé, *La réalité concrète et la dialectique*, Paris, Vrin, 1931, 132pp, [8°R.38301].

Revue de métaphysique et de morale, 38, no. 3, 1931, p.277-510. Special number commemorating the centenary of Hegel's death. Published as a separate volume under the title *Etudes sur Hegel*, Paris, Armand Colin, [4°R.3757]. The following articles are included (pagination of volume):

— Croce, B., 'Un cercle vicieux dans la critique de la philosophie hégélienne', p.1-8;
— Hartmann, Nicolaï, 'Hegel et le problème de la dialectique du réel', p.9-40;
— Andler, Charles, 'Le fondement du savoir dans la "Phénoménologie de l'Esprit" de Hegel', p.41-64;
— Basch, Victor, 'Des origines et des fondements de l'esthétique de Hegel', p.65-90; reprinted in Basch's *Essais d'esthétique, de philosophie et de littérature*, Paris, Alcan, 1934, p.89-130.
— Berthelot, René, 'Goethe et Hegel', p.91-136;
— Guéroult, M., 'Le jugement de Hegel sur l'antithétique de la raison pure', p.157-163;
— Vermeil, Edmond, 'La pensée politique de Hegel', p.165-234.
Revue philosophique de la France et de l'étranger, novembre-décembre 1931. Special issue commemorating the Centenary of Hegel's death; the main articles are as follows:
— Wahl, Jean, 'Hegel et Kierkegaard', p.321-380. Reprinted in *Verhandlungen des 3. Hegelkongresses vom 19. bis 23. April 1933 in Rom*, Tübingen & Haarlem, 1934, p.250-268, and in his *Etudes kierkegaardiennes*, Paris, Vrin, 1938, p.159-171.
— Basch, Victor, 'De la philosophie politique de Hegel, à propos d'un ouvrage récent', p.381-408;
— Koyré, Alexandre, 'Note sur la langue et la terminologie hégélienne', p.409-439. Reprinted in his *Etudes d'histoire de la pensée philsophique*, 1971.
Sfard, David, *Du rôle de l'idée de contradiction chez Hegel*, Nancy, R. Poncelet, 1931, 157pp, [8°R.39436]. Thesis for doctorat de l'Université, Nancy.
Koyré, Alexandre, 'Rapport sur l'état des études hégéliennes en France', *Revue d'histoire de la philosophie*, avril-juin 1931, p.147-171. Also printed in *Verhandlungen des 1. Hegelkongresses vom 22. bis 25. April in Haag*, Tübingen & Haarlem, 1931, p.106-126. Reprinted in his *Etudes d'histoire de la pensée philsophique*, 1971.
Kuiper, Vincenz M., 'Le "réalisme" de Hegel', *Revue des sciences philosophiques et théologiques*, 20, no. 2, 1931, p.233-258.
Lenoir, Raymond, 'Le Centenaire de Hegel', *Revue d'histoire de la philosophie*, juillet-decembre 1931, p.352-363.

1932

Alain, (pseudonym for Emile-Auguste Chartier), *Idées. Introduction à la philosophie: Platon, Descartes, Hegel, Auguste Comte*, Paris, P. Hartmann, 1932, 304pp, [8°Z.Don 596 (18)]. Reprinted in 1939, and again by Flammarion in 1967.
Andler, Charles, *La Vie de Lucien Herr*, Paris, Rieder, 1932, 338pp.
Berthelot, René, *Science et philosophie chez Goethe, 2. Goethe et Hegel*, Paris, Alcan, 1932, 188pp.
Bréhier, Emile, *Histoire de la philosophie*, vol. 2, Paris, Alcan, 1932.
Chevrillon, A, *Taine, formation de sa pensée*, Paris, 1932.
Nizan, Paul, *Les Chiens de garde*, Paris, Rieder, 1932. Reprinted Paris, Maspéro, 1971.
Forest, Aimé, 'L'hégélianisme en France', *Rivista di filosofia neoscolastica*, 23, 1932, p.118-130.
Wahl, Jean, 'Commémoration du centenaire de la mort de Hegel dans les revues philosophiques allemandes et françaises', *Revue d'Allemagne*, 6, 1932, p.268.

1933

Marx, Karl, 'Critique de la dialectique hégélienne', tr. H. Lefebvre & N. Guterman, *Avant-poste*, juin 1933, p.32-39; août 1933, p.110-116, [8°Z.26403].

1934

Cornu, Auguste, *Karl Marx, l'homme et l'oeuvre. De l'hégélianisme au matérialisme historique*, Paris, Alcan, 1934, 428pp, [8°M.24527]. Doctoral thesis, Paris, originally entitled 'La jeunesse de Karl Marx'.

Cornu, Auguste, *Moses Hess et la gauche hégélienne*, Paris, Presses Universitaires de France, 1934, 124pp, [8°R.43245].

Croce, Benedetto, 'La "mort de l'art" dans le système hégélien', *Revue de métaphysique et de morale*, 41, no. 1, 1934, p.l-11.

Koyré, Alexandre, 'Hegel à Jena. A propos de publications récentes', *Revue philosophique de la France et de l'étranger*, 59, vol. 118, 1934, p.274-283. Reprinted in *Revue d'histoire et de philosophie religieuses*, 15, 1935, p.420-458, and in his *Etudes d'histoire de la pensée philosophique*, 1971.

Loewith, Karl, 'L'achèvement de la philosophie classique par Hegel et sa dissolution chez Marx et Kierkegaard', *Recherches philosophiques*, 4, 1934-5, p.232-267.

Europe, 15 mai 1934, p.5-37, text of a debate on dialectics, as follows:
— Eastman, Max, 'Contre la dialectique marxiste', p.5-19;
— Simpson, Herman, 'Pour la dialectique marxiste', p.19-34;
— Eastman, Max, & Simpson, Herman, 'Pourquoi existe la dia-lectique', p.34-37, an exchange of letters.

1935

A la lumière du marxisme, essais, Paris, Editions Sociales Internationales, 1935, [8°R.41763]. A collection of essays, of which those concerning Hegelian dialectics are as follows:
— Maublanc, René, 'Hegel et Marx', p.189-232;
— Labérenne, Paul, 'Le matérialisme dialectique et les sciences', p.233-261;
— Friedmann, Georges, 'Matérialisme dialectique et action réciproque', p.262-284;
— Baby, Jean, 'Le matérialisme historique', p.285-310.

Marx, Karl, *Œuvres philosophiques*, tr. J. Molitor, vol. 4, Paris, Costes, 1935, [8°R.35356 (4)]. Contains 'Critique de la philosophie de l'état de Hegel', p.17-259.

Maublanc, René, *La philosophie du marxisme et l'enseignement officiel*, Paris, Bureau d'Editions, 1935, 72pp, collection 'Les Cahiers de contre-enseignement prolétarien', [8°R.40414 (19)].

Cornu, Auguste, 'Karl Marx et la pensée romantique allemande: le problème de l'action', *Europe*, 15 octobre 1935, p.199-216.

Flechtheim, Ossip Kurt, 'La fonction de la peine dans la théorie du droit de Hegel', *Revue internationale de la théorie du droit*, 10, 1935, p.189-197.

Hyppolite, Jean, 'Les travaux de jeunesse de Hegel d'après des ouvrages récents', *Revue de métaphysique et de morale*, no.42, 1935, p.399-426; p.549-578.

Loewith, Karl, 'La conciliation hégélienne', *Recherches philosophiques*, 5, 1935, p.393-404.

Moré, Marcel, 'Les années d'apprentissage de Karl Marx. A propos d'un livre récent', *Esprit*, avril 1935 - janvier 1936. A series of articles subtitled as follows: 'Avant-propos', avril 1935, p.15-30; 'La mélodie rocailleuse', juin 1935, p.355-372; 'Critique de l'état hégélien', septembre 1935, p.752-772; 'Vers le matérialisme historique: L'humanisme communiste', octobre 1935, p.47-70; 'La pensée de Marx et nous', janvier 1936, p.552-568.

Salomon-Delatour, G., 'Comte ou Hegel?' *Revue positiviste internationale*, 1935, 5-6, p.220-227; 1936, 3, p.110-118.

1936

Guterman, Norbert & Lefebvre, Henri, *La Conscience mystifiée*, Paris, Gallimard, 1936, [8°Z.25678 (14)].

Michael Kelly

Koyré, Alexandre, 'Hegel en Russie', *Monde slave*, n.s. 13, vol. 2, 1936, p.215-248; p.321-364. Reprinted in his *Etudes sur l'histoire de la pensée philosophique en Russie*, Paris, Vrin, 1951.
Rondet, Henri, 'Hegel et le christianisme, réflexions théologiques', *Recherches de science religieuse*, 26, 1936, p.257-296; p.419-453.

1937

Hook, Sydney, *Pour comprendre Marx*, Paris, Gallimard, 1937, [8°R.43692].

1938

Lénine, V. I., *Cahiers sur la dialectique de Hegel*, Paris, Gallimard, 1938, [4°R.5021]. Translated and with a lengthy introduction by Henri Lefebvre and Norbert Guterman. Reprinted in 1967 by Gallimard in the collection 'Idées'.
Mougin, Henri, *Pierre Leroux*, Paris, 1938, 297pp.
Wahl, Jean, *Etudes kierkegaardiennes*, Paris, Editions Montaigne, 1938. Contains section 'La lutte contre le hégélianisme', p.86-171. 2nd edition, Paris, Vrin, 1949, 647pp.
Hyppolite, Jean, 'Vie et prise de conscience de la vie dans la philosophie hégélienne d'Iéna', *Revue de métaphysique et de morale*, 45, 1938, p.45-61.

1939

Lefebvre, Henri, *Le Matérialisme dialectique*, Paris, Alcan, 1939, [8°R.40994 (21)]. Reprinted by Presses Universitaires de France in 1947 and many times subsequently.
Précis d'Histoire du Parti communiste (bolchévik) de l'URSS, Paris, 1939. French translation of the 'Short course' of which the chapter 'Le matérialisme dialectique et historique' is generally attributed to Stalin.
Croce, Benedetto, 'La place de Hegel dans l'histoire de la philosophie', *Revue de métaphysique et de morale*, 46, no. 2, 1939, p.211-224.
Hyppolite, Jean, 'La Signification de la Révolution française dans la "Phénoménologie" de Hegel', *Revue philosophique de la France et de l'étranger*, septembre-décembre 1939, p.320-352.
Stern, Alfred, 'Hegel et les idées de 1789', *Revue philosophique de la France et de l'étranger*, septembre-décembre 1939, p.353-363.

1940

Delbos, Victor, *De Kant aux post-kantiens*, Paris, Editions Montaigne, 1940, 208pp.
Bertrand, Pierre, 'Les sens du tragique et du destin dans la dialectique hégélienne', *Revue de métaphysique et de morale*, avril 1940, p.165-186.

1941

Mueller, Fernand-Lucien, *La Pensée contemporaine en Italie et l'influence de Hegel*, Geneva, Pr. Kundig, 1941, xviii-345pp, [4°θ.Gen.lettr.16]. Thesis at the University of Geneva.

1942

Thomas, André, 'La pensée allemande et la formation de l'Europe: III. L'idéalisme romantique', *Bulletin de l'Ouest*, 14, 15 octobre 1942, p.159-162.
Badelle, J., 'Foi religieuse et connaissance philosophique. A propos de Hegel "Glauben und Wissen"', *Revue philosophique de la France et de l'étranger*, 67, vol 133, no. 79, 194-243, p.68-83.

1943

Sartre, Jean-Paul, *L'être et le néant*, Paris, Gallimard, 1943, 722pp.

SECTION THREE

PUBLICATIONS ON HEGEL IN FRENCH 1945-1964

The list is a substantially complete inventory of publications relating to Hegel published in French between 1945 and 1964. Entries are listed in year order, and alphabetically within each year, with articles grouped separately in each year, after books and collections of papers.

1945

Droz, Jacques, *Le Libéralisme rhénan 1815-1848. Contribution à l'histoire du libéralisme allemand*, Paris, Nouvelles Editions Latines, 1945, xviii-462pp.

Niel, Henri, *De la médiation dans la philosophie de Hegel*, Paris, Aubier, 1945, 376pp.

Grégoire, Franz, 'Hegel et la primauté respective de la raison et du rationnel', *Revue néoscolastique de philosophie*, vol 43, 1940-1945, p.252-264.

Merleau-Ponty, Maurice, 'Une conférence de J. Hyppolite. L'existentialisme chez Hegel', *Les Temps modernes*, 1, no. 7, 1945 p.1311-1319. Reprinted in his *Sens et non-sens*, Paris, Nagel, 1948.

Sartre, Jean-Paul, 'Matérialisme et révolution', *Les Temps modernes*, 1, no. 9, 1945, p.1537-1563; no. 10, 1945, p.1-32.

1946

Angrand, Cécile, *Le matérialisme dialectique*, Paris, Editions Sociales, 1946, 'Cours de l'université nouvelle'.

Hyppolite, Jean-Gaston, *Genèse et structure de la Phénoménologie de l'Esprit de Hegel*, Paris, Aubier, 1946, 592pp.

Cornu, Auguste, 'Le mouvement encyclopédique français et la gauche hégélienne', *Revue germanique*, 1, 1946, p.402-416.

Grégoire, Franz, 'Hegel et l'universelle contradiction', *Revue philosophique de Louvain*, 44, no. 1, 1946, p.36-73.

Hyppolite, Jean, 'L'existence dans la phénoménologie de Hegel', *Etudes germaniques*, 1, 1946, p.131-141.'

Kojève, Alexandre, 'Hegel, Marx et le christianisme', *Critique*, no. 3-4, 1946, p.339-366.

Mougin, Henri, 'Hegel et le neveu de Rameau', *Europe*, août 1946, p.1-11.

1947

Carré, Jean-Marie, *Les écrivains français et le mirage allemand 1800-1940*, Paris, Boivin, 1947.

Grégoire, Franz, *Aux sources de la pensée de Marx: Hegel, Feuerbach*, Louvain, Editions de l'Institut Supérieur de Philosophie, and Paris, Vrin, 1947, 205pp.

Jdanov, A. A., *Sur la philosophie, la littérature et la musique*, Paris, Editions de la Nouvelle critique, 1947.

Kojève, Alexandre, *Introduction à la lecture de Hegel*, Paris, Gallimard, 1947. Edited by Raymond Queneau. Published in the collection 'Tel', 1979.

Lefebvre, Henri, *A la lumière du matérialisme dialectique. 1. Logique formelle, logique dialectique*, Paris, Editions Sociales, 1947, 291p. Reprinted as *Logique formelle, logique dialectique*, Paris, Editions Anthropos, 1969.

Lefebvre, Henri, *La Pensée de Karl Marx*, Paris, Bordas, 1947, collection 'Pour connaître la pensée de', 254pp.

Mougin, Henri, *La Sainte famille existentialiste*, Paris, Editions Sociales, 1947, 192pp.

Zévaès, André, *De l'introduction du marxisme en France*, Paris, Rivière, 1947.

A. A., 'Hegel était-il marxiste?', *Revue internationale*, 12, 1947.

Alain (pseud Emile Chartier), 'Les difficultés de la phénoménalogie de Hegel', *Mercure de France*, 301, 1947, p.35-46.

Althusser, Louis, 'Introduction à la lecture de Hegel', *Cahiers du sud*, 34, no.286, 1947, p.1057-1059.

Derins, F., 'Etudes hégéliennes', *La Nef*, 4, 1947, p.137-139.

Fessard, Gaston, 'Deux interprètes de la Phénoménologie de Hegel: Jean Hyppolite et Alexandre Kojève', *Études*, décembre 1947, p.368-373.

Forest, A., 'Etudes sur Hegel', *Revue Thomiste*, no. 2, 1947, p.372-376.

Grégoire, Franz, 'Hegel et la divinité de l'Etat', *Actes du IIIe congrès des sociétés de philosophie de langue française*, Louvain & Paris, 1947, p.247-253.

Grégoire, Franz, 'L'Etat et la vie spirituelle de l'homme selon Hegel', *Tijdschrift voor Philosophie*, vol. 9, no. 4, 1947, p.637-660.

Hyppolite, Jean, 'L'aliénation hégélienne et la critique', *Atti des congresso internazionale di filosofia, Roma 1946*, vol 1, Milano, Castelli, 1947, p.53-55.

Hyppolite, Jean, 'Situation de l'homme dans la phénoménologie hégélienne', *LesTemps modernes*, 2, no.19, 1947, p.1276-1289.

Jdanov, A. A., 'Sur l'histoire de la philosophie', *Europe*, novembre 1947, p.40-66. Reprinted in *Cahiers du communisme*, décembre 1947, p.1301-1325.

Lacroix, Jean, 'Hegel et Marx', *Le Monde*, 23 octobre 1947.

Niel, Henri, 'L'interprétation de Hegel'. *Critique*, 18, novembre 1947, p.426-437.

1948

Cahiers internationaux de sociologie, 1948, special issue on Young Marx, including among others the following articles:
— B. Bettelheim, 'Idéologie et réalité sociale', p.119-134;
— M. Dufrenne, 'Histoire et historicité', p. 97-118;
— J. Hyppolite, 'La conception hégélienne de l'Etat et la critique de Karl Marx', p.120-141.

Cornu, Auguste, *Karl Marx et la pensée moderne. Contribution à l'étude de la formation du marxisme*, Paris, Editions Sociales. 1948.

Gilson, Etienne, *L'Etre et l'essence*, Paris, Vrin, 1948, 329pp.

Hyppolite, Jean, *Introduction à la philosophie de l'histoire de Hegel*, Paris, Rivière, 1948, 98pp. Reprinted Paris, Editions du Seuil, 1983, collection 'Points'.

Klossowski, Pierre, *'Les Méditations bibliques' de Hamann. Avec une étude de Hegel*, Paris, Minuit, 1948.

Lefebvre, Henri, *Le Marxisme*, Paris, Presses Universitaires de France, 1948, collection 'Que sais-je'. Much reprinted.

Lukács, Georges, *Existentialisme ou marxisme?*, Paris, Nagel, 1948. Reprinted 1961.

Merleau-Ponty, Maurice, *Sens et non-sens*, Paris, Nagel, 1948. Contains essay 'L'existentialisme chez Hegel'.

Pensa, Mario, *Le Logos hégélien*, Lausanne, F. Rougé, 1948.

Plekhanov, G., *Les Questions fondamentales du Marxisme*, Paris, Editions Sociales, 1948. Contains essay 'La philosophie de Hegel'.

Belaval, Yvon, 'Approches de Hegel', *Etudes germaniques*, 3, 1948, p.80-88.

Canguilhem, Georges, 'Hegel en France', *Revue d'histoire et de philosphie religieuse*, Strasbourg, no. 4, 1948-9, p.282-297.

Michael Kelly

Cornu, Auguste, 'L'idee d'aliénation chez Hegel, Feuerbach et Karl Marx', *La Pensée*, mars-avril 1948, p.65-75.
Dufrenne, Mikel, 'Actualité de Hegel', *Esprit*, septembre 1948, p.396-408. Reprinted in his *Jalons*, The Hague, Nijhoff, 1966, p.70-83.
Gandillac, Maurice de, 'Ambiguïté hégélienne', *Dieu vivant*, xi, 1948, p.125-144.
Hyppolite, Jean, 'De la structure philosophique du *Capital* et de quelques présupposés de l'œuvre de Marx', *Bulletin de la société française de philosophie*, 42, 1948, p.171-190.
Kanapa, Jean, 'Chronique philosophique: Un débat sur la logique en URSS, la Logique d'Henri Lefebvre, les interprètes de Hegel', *La Pensée*, mars-avril 1948, p.111-121.
Klossowski, Pierre, 'Hegel et le mage du nord, Johann Georg Hamann', *Temps modernes*, 35, 1948, p.234-238.
Tran-Duc-Thao, 'La "Phénoménologie de l'Esprit" et son contenu réel', *Les Temps modernes*, septembre 1948, 492-519.

1949

Cresson, André & René Serreau, *Hegel, sa vie, son oeuvre*, Paris, Presses Universitaires de France, 1949, in the collection 'Philosophes', 136pp. 4th edition 1963.
Lacroix, Jean, *Marxisme, existentialisme, personnalisme*, Paris, Presses Universitaires de France, 1949. 124pp.
Armand, Felix & Auguste Cornu, 'Critique et autocritique', *La Pensée*, septembre-octobre 1949, p.84-88.
Bonnel, P., 'Hegel et Marx à la lumière de quelques travaux contemporains', *Critique*, vol. 5, no. 34, 1949, p.221-232.
Darbon, Michel, 'Hégélianisme, marxisme, existentialisme', *Etudes philosophiques*, n.s. 4, no. 3-4, 1949, p.346-370.
Dhanis, Ed., 'En marge d'un cours sur Hegel et Feuerbach', *Gregorianum*, 30, no. 4, 1949, p.574-596.
Fessard, Gaston, 'L'actualité prophétique de Hamann', *Etudes*, vol. 263, 1949, p.116-119.
Grégoire, Franz, 'La raison de la valeur de l'état selon Hegel', *Proceedings of the Tenth International Congress of Philosophy* (Amsterdam), 1949, p.1180-1182.
Lefebvre, Henri, 'Autocritique: Contribution à l'effort d'éclaircissement idéologique', *La Nouvelle critique*, mars 1949, p.41-57.
Lukács, Georg, 'Les nouveaux problèmes de la recherche hégélienne', *Bulletin de la société française de philosophie*, 43, no, 2, 1949, p.53-72.
Vexliard, A., 'Tendances actuelles de la philosophie en U.R.S.S.', *Critique*, vol. 5, no. 33, 1949, p.139-147.
Waelhens, Alphonse de, 'Jean Hyppolite, Introduction à la philosophie de l'histoire de Hegel', *Revue philosophique de Louvain*, 47, 1949, p.147-150.

1950

Weil, Eric, *Logique de la philosophie*, Paris, Vrin, 1950, xii-442pp. Reprinted 1953.
Weil, Eric, *Hegel et l'état*, Paris, Vrin, 1950, 116pp. 6th edition 1985.
Bottigelli, E., 'A propos du retour à Hegel', *La Nouvelle critique*, décembre 1950, p.73-81.
Commission de critique du cercle des philosophes communistes, 'Le retour à Hegel: dernier mot du révisionnisme universitaire', *La Nouvelle critique*, novembre 1950, p.43-54.
Forest, Aimé, 'Chronique d'histoire de la philosophie', *La Revue Thomiste*, no. 1, 1950, p.231-241.
Plekhanov, Georges, 'La signification de Hegel', *La Revue internationale*, 6, no. 22, 1950, p.86-104.
Weil, Eric, 'Hegel et son interprétation communiste', *Critique*, octobre 1950, p.91-93.

1951

Amar, André, *Les Grands courants de la pensée européenne: Introduction à la pensée phénoménologique*, Paris, Cours de droit, 1951.

Cornu, Auguste, *Essai de critique marxiste*, Paris, Editions sociales, 1951, 183pp.

Lubac, Henri de, *Affrontements mystiques*, Paris, Costard, 1951, 214pp.

Tran Duc Thao, *Phénoménologie et matérialisme dialectique*, Paris, Editions Minh Tan, 1951, 368pp.

Hyppolite, Jean, 'Aliénation et objectivation: à propos du livre de Lukács sur la jeunesse de Hegel', *Etudes germaniques*, 6, 1951, no. 2, p.117-124; 7, 1952, no. 1, p.37-43.

Hyppolite, Jean, 'E. Weil, Hegel et l'Etat', *Revue de métaphysique et de morale*, 56, no. 4, 1951, p.446.

Lefebvre, Henri, 'Lettre sur Hegel', *La Nouvelle critique*, janvier 1951, p.99-104.

Minder, Robert, '"Herrlichkeit" chez Hegel ou le monde des pères souabes', *Etudes germaniques*, 6, 1951, p.275-290.

Petronievics, Branislav, 'Les trois dialectiques', *Revue philosophique de la France et de l'étranger*, no. 76, 1951, p.530-542.

Waelhens, Alphonse de, 'E. Weil, Hegel et l'Etat', *Revue philosophique de Louvain*, 49, no. 22, 1951, p.471-473.

1952

Asveld, Paul, *Hegel, réformateur religieux, 1793-1796*, Louvain, 1952.

Eckles, Larry Edward, 'La fortune intellectuelle de Hegel en France au dix-neuvième siècle, introduction méthodologique et historique (1817-1847)', Unpublished thesis for Doctorat d'Université, Faculté des Lettres de l'Université de Paris, 1952, 279pp.

Revue internationale de la philosophie (Bruxelles), no. 19, fasc. 1, 1952. Special number on Hegel including the following items in French:
— Croce, Benedetto, 'Hegel et l'origine de la dialectique', p.12-26.
— Hyppolite, Jean, 'Essai sur la Logique de Hegel', p.35-49.

Aebli, M, 'Critique de la construction marxiste et hégélienne de l'histoire. L'homme et l'histoire', *Actes du VIe congrès des sociétés de philosophie de langue française*, Paris, Presses Universitaires de France, 1952, p.281-290.

Asveld, Paul, 'Hegel réformateur religieux', pamphlet printed by Publications universitaires de Louvain, 1952, 23pp.

Dumas, J., 'Politique hégélienne'. L'aspect politique de l'hegelianisme à la lumière de quelques travaux récents', *Vie intellectuelle*, 20, no. 8-9, 1952, p.124-131.

1953

Asveld, Paul, *La Pensée religieux du jeune Hegel, liberté et aliénation*, Louvain, Publications universitaires, & Paris, Desclée de Brouwer, 1953, 244pp.

Grégoire, Franz, *L'Attitude hégélienne devant l'existence*, Louvain, Editions de l'Institut Supérieur de Philosophie, 1953, 46pp.

Hyppolite, Jean, *Logique et existence, essai sur la Logique de Hegel*, Paris, Presses Universitaires de France, 1953, 250pp.

Breton, Stanislas, 'La dialectique de la conscience dans la phénoménologie de l'esprit de Hegel', *Euntes docete*, 6, no. 3, 1953, p.323-360.

Fetscher, Iring, 'Individu et communauté dans la philosophie de Hegel', *Actes du XI congrès international de philosophie*, Amsterdam & Louvain, 1953, p.125-130.

Fréville, Jean, 'La vie de Karl Marx', *Cahiers du communisme*, avril 1953, p.503-512.

Grégoire, Franz, 'L'attitude hégélienne devant l'existence', *Revue philosophique de Louvain*, 51, no. 30, 1953, p.187-232.

Hyppolite, Jean, 'La critique hégélienne de la réflexion kantienne', *Kant-Studien*, no 45, 1953-54, p.83-95.

Niel, Henri, 'De Hegel à Marx', *La Vie intellectuelle*, 21, no. 3, 1953, p.69-74.

Ouy, Achille, 'Connaissance de Hegel', *Mercure de France*, no. 1078, 1953, p.355-368.
Wahl, Jean, 'Une interprétation de la logique de Hegel. A propos de l'ouvrage de J. Hyppolite: *Logique et existence*', *Critique*, no. 79, 1953, p.1050-1071.

1954

Arvon, Henri, *Aux sources de l'existentialisme, Max Stirner*, Paris, Presses Universitaires de France, 1954, 188pp.
Houang, François, *Le Néo-hégélianisme en Angleterre: la philosophie de Bernard Bosanquet*, Paris, Vrin, 1954, 232pp. A doctoral thesis originally entitled 'De l'humanisme à l'absolutisme. Essai sur l'évolution de la pensée religieuse du neo-hégélien anglais Bernard Bosanquet (1848-1932)'.
Marrou, Henri, *De la connaissance historique*, Paris, Seuil, 1954.
Bottigelli, Emile, 'Comment Lénine lit Hegel', *La Pensée*, septembre-octobre 1954, p.110-114.
Calvez, Jean-Yves, 'L'âge d'or. Essai sur le destin de la "belle âme" chez Novalis et Hegel', *Etudes germaniques*, 9, 1954, p.112-127.
Cornu, Auguste, 'Une étude sur Hegel', *La Pensée*, mars-avril 1954, 116-118.
Desanti, Jean, 'Hegel, est-il le père de l'existentialisme', *La Nouvelle critique*, juin 1954, p.91-109; juillet-août 1954, p.163-187.
Fessard, Gaston, 'Hegel: Premières publications', *Etudes*, vol. 281, 1954, p.267.
Lacroix, Jean, 'La signification de la pensée de Hegel', *Le Monde*, 3 juin 1954.
Patri, Aimé, 'En relisant l'Esthétique de Hegel', *Paru*, 10, nos 80-81, 1954, p.132-136.
Waelhens, Alphonse de, 'Phénoménologie husserlienne et phénoménologie hégélienne', *Revue philosophique de Louvain*, no. 52, 1954, p.234-249. Reprinted in his *Existence et signification*, Paris & Louvain, Nauwelaerts, 1958.

1955

Barth, Karl, *Hegel*, tr. J. Carrère, Paris & Neuchâtel, Delachaux & Niestlé, 1955, 56pp.
Cornu, Auguste, *Karl Marx et Friedrich Engels*, vol. 1, Paris, Presses Universitaires de France, 1955.
Hyppolite, Jean, *Etudes sur Marx et Hegel*, Paris, Rivière, 1955, 204pp.
Lénine, V.I., *Cahiers philosophiques*, tr. Lida Vernant & Emile Bottigelli, Paris, Editions sociales, 1955.
Merleau-Ponty, Maurice, *Les Aventures de la dialectique*, Paris, Gallimard, 1955.
Mao Tse-tung, *Œuvres choisies*, Paris, Editions Sociales, 1955. Contains essays 'A propos de la contradiction' and 'A propos de la pratique'.
Niel, Henri, *Philosophies chrétiennes*, Paris, 1955. Contains essay 'Hégélianisme et christianisme'.
Verneaux, R., *L'Histoire de la philosophie et de la métaphysique*, Paris, Desclée de Brouwer, 1955. Contains chapter 'L'essence du scepticisme chez Hegel'.
Bottigelli, Emile, 'Le chemin de Marx', *Nouvelle critique*, 62, février 1955, p.17-21.
Châtelet, François, 'Le marxisme est-il un prophétisme?', *Nouvelle critique*, 70, décembre 1955, p.64-81.
Cottier, (Georges) M. M., o.p., 'Chronique hégélienne', *Revue thomiste*, 3, 1955, p.670-688.
Deucalion 5, (Neuchâtel), 40e cahier, octobre 1955. Special number entitled 'Etudes hégéliennes', with the following articles:
— Kojève, Alexandre, 'Le concept et le temps', p.11-20;
— Bataille, Georges, 'Hegel, la mort et le sacrifice', p.21-43;
— Bataille, Georges & Raymond Queneau, 'La critique des fonde-ments de la dialectique hégélienne', p.45-60;
— Queneau, Raymond, 'Dialectique hégélienne et séries de Fourier', p.61-76.
— Wahl, Jean, 'A propos de l'Introduction à la Phénoménologie de Hegel par A. Kojève', p.77-100;
— Weil, Eric, 'La morale de Hegel', p.101-118.

Gaide, Dom Gilles, & Roger Grampon & Adrien Laurie, 'Le rôle des martyrs dans l'histoire', *Témoignages*, 49, mai 1955, p.193-221. Three pieces, 'Introduction' (p.193-198); 'Hegel ou les insuffisances de l'histoire' (G. Gaide, p.199-214); 'Marx ou la contradiction de l'histoire' (R. Crampon, p.215-221).

Grégoire, Franz, 'Une semi-légende: la "divinité" de l'Etat chez Hegel', *Bulletin de l'Académie royale de Belgique. Classe des lettres et des sciences morales et politiques*, 5e série, t. 41, 6, 1955, p.315-329. Reprinted in his *Etudes hégéliennes* (1958).

Lukács, Georges, 'Les Manuscrits de 1844 et la formation du marxisme', *Nouvelle critique*, 66, juin 1955, p.31-47.

Niel, Henri, 'La philosophie du travail chez Hegel et chez Marx, choix de textes', *Lumière et Vie*, 20, 1955, p.23-48.

Ramier, Claude, 'Hegel et l'histoire de la philosophie', *La Pensée*, 64, novembre-décembre 1955, p.92-97.

Ricœur, Paul, 'Philosophie et ontologie. 1. Retour à Hegel', *Esprit*, 23, no. 8, 1955, p.1378-1391.

Sapienta Aquinatis. Communicationes IV. congressus Thomistici internationalis. Romae, 13-17 Septembris 1955, 2 vols, Rome, Officium Libri Catholici, 1955. Volume 1 contains the following papers in French:
— Chaix-Ruy, J., 'Hegel et Saint Thomas: Dialectique et logique', p.212-221;
— Garrigou-Lagrange, R., 'Dialectique hégélienne et métaphysique thomiste', p.271-282;
— Grégoire, F., 'Thèmes hégéliens et dépassements thomistes', p.282-292.

Sebag, Lucien, 'Marx, Feuerbach et la critique de la religion', *Nouvelle critique*, 64, avril 1955, p.17-38.

1956

Calvez, Jean-Yves, *La pensée de Karl Marx*, Paris, Editions du Seuil, 1956. Contains chapter 'La dialectique'.

Eyselé, Charles, ed., *Aspects de la dialectique*, Paris, Desclée de Brouwer, 1956.

Fessard, Gaston, *La Dialectique des Exercices Spirituels de saint Ignace de Loyola*, Paris, 1956, 368pp.

Merleau-Ponty, Maurice, editor, *Les philosophes célèbres*, Paris, Mazenod, 1956, 460pp. Contains chapter by Eric Weil, 'Hegel', p.258-265.

Niel, Henri, *Philosophies de l'histoire*, Paris, Fayard, 1956. Contains chapter 'Hégélianisme et histoire'.

Varet, Gilbert, *Manuel de bibliographie philosophique*, Paris, Presses Universitaires de France, 1956. Contains section 'Hegel posthume'.

Amar, André, 'Les deux sources de la philosophie hégélienne', *Evidences*, 54, 1956, p.1-4.

Besse, Guy, 'Les "Cahiers philosophiques" de Lénine', *La Pensée*, janvier-février 1956, p.85-94.

Bataille, Georges, 'Hegel, l'homme et l'histoire', *Paru*, 96, janvier 1956, p.21-23; 97, février 1956, p.1-14.

Garaudy, Roger, 'A propos des "Cahiers philosophiques" de Lénine', *Cahiers du communisme*, janvier 1956, p.131-155.

Lapierre, J.-W., 'Hegel, Barth et l'homme moderne', *Semeur*, 8, 1956, p.185-187.

Niel, Henri, 'Hégélianisme et histoire', *Recherches et débats*, 17, 1956, p.20-46.

1957

Arvon, Henri, *Feuerbach ou la transformation du sacré*, Paris, Presses Universitaires de France, 1957, 188pp.

Lefebvre, Henri, *La Pensée de Lénine*, Paris, Bordas, 1957, in the collection 'Pour connaître'.

Marietti, Angèle, *La Pensée de Hegel. Suivi d'une étude de Jean Wahl*, Paris, Bordas, 1957, in the collection 'Pour connaître'. Jean Wahl's essay is entitled 'Hegel et Heidegger', p.185-195.

Naville, Pierre, *Le nouveau Léviathan. 1. De l'aliénation à la jouissance*, Paris, Rivière, 1957.

Rubel, Maximillien, *Karl Marx. Essai de biographie intellectuelle*, Paris, Rivière, 1957, 464pp.

Bonnel, P., 'Hegel et Marx', *La Revue socialiste*, 110, 1957, p.314-325; 111, 1957, p.428-440.

Caire, Guy, *L'Aliénation dans les œuvres de jeunesse de Marx*, Aix-en-Provence, La Pensée Universitaire, 1957. 130pp.

Grégoire, Franz, 'La dialectique hégélienne de l'être, du néant et du devenir', *Revue de métaphysique et de morale*, 1957, no. 1, p.84-95.

Lefebvre, Henri, 'Le marxisme et la pensée française', *Les Temps modernes*, 13, 1957, p.104-137.

Lukács, Georg, 'Qu'est-ce que le marxisme orthodoxe?', *Arguments*, 1, 1957, no. 3, p.1-17.

Maritain, Jacques, 'La dialectique de Hegel', *Nouvelle revue française*, no. 49, 1957, p.19-30; no. 50, 1957, p.228-241.

Munzer, T., 'A propos de Lukács', *Arguments*, 1, 1957, no. 3, p.17-22.

Sartre, Jean-Paul, 'Questions de méthode', *Les Temps modernes*, 13, 1957, p.338-417; p.658-698.

1958

Cornu, Auguste, *Karl Marx et Friedrich Engels*, vol. 2, Paris, Presses Universitaires de France, 1958.

Grégoire, Franz, *Etudes hégéliennes, les points capitaux du système*, Louvain & Paris, Nauwelaerts, 1958, ix-411pp.

Lefebvre, Henri, *Problèmes actuels du marxisme*, Paris, Presses Universitaires de France, 1958.

Verneaux, Roger, *Histoire de la philosophie moderne*, Paris, Beauchesne, 1958, in the 'Cours de philosophie thomiste'.

Teyssèdre, Bernard, *L'Esthétique de Hegel*, Paris, Presses Universitaires de France, 1958, 104pp. Reprinted frequently.

Birault, Henri, 'L'onto-théologique hégélienne et la dialectique', *Tijdschrift voor philosophie*, 20, 1958, no. 4, p.646-723.

Heidegger, Martin, 'Hegel et les Grecs', *Cahiers du sud*, 45, no.349, 1958, p.355-368.

Sève, Lucien, 'Henri Lefebvre et la dialectique chez Marx', *La Nouvelle critique*, 94, mars 1958, p.55-89.

Taminiaux, Jacques, 'La pensée esthétique du jeune Hegel', *Revue philosophique de Louvain*, 56, 1958, p.222-250.

Teyssèdre, Bernard, 'Les soirées parisiennes de Hegel. D'après une documentation traduite avec l'aide de Arnim Raith', *Revue d'esthétique*, 11, 1958, nos 1-2, p.40-74.

1959

Cottier, Georges M.M., *L'athéisme du jeune Marx: ses origines hégéliennes*, Paris, Vrin, 1959, 384pp.

Morin, Edgar, *Autocritique*, Paris, Julliard, 1959. Reprinted Paris, Editions du Seuil, 1975, in the collection 'Points'.

Wahl, Jean, *Commentaire de la logique de Hegel*, Paris, Centre de Documentation Universitaire, 1959, 'Les cours de la Sorbonne', 160pp.

Wahl, Jean, *La logique de Hegel comme phénoménologie*, Paris, SEDES, 1959, 'Les cours de la Sorbonne', 160pp. Frequently reprinted.

Fetscher, Iring, 'Hegel et le marxisme', *Archives de philosophie*, 22, 1959, no. 3, p.323-368; 23, 1960, no. 4, p.522-572.

Hayen, André, 'Hegel et Blondel. A propos d'un livre récent', *Revue philosophique de Louvain*, serie 3, no. 55, 1959, p.342-350.

Langlois, Jean, 'Note sur Hegel et le principe de contradiction', *Sciences ecclésiastiques*, xi, 1959, p.99-110.

Marc, A., 'Marx et Hegel', *Archives de philosophie*, 15, 1959, no. 2, p.145-173.

Regnier, P. M., 'La philosophie hégélienne et l'évolution de l'humanité', *Archives de philosophie*, 22, 1959, no. 1, p.115-119.

Sève, Lucien, 'Panorama de la philosophie française contemporaine', *La Pensée*, 88, nov-déc 1959, p.51-80; 89, jan-fév 1960, p.75-89; 90, mars-avril 1960, p.56-76; 91, mai-juin 1960, 67-90; 92, juillet-août 1960, p.34-68.

Waelhens, Alphonse de, 'Réflexions sur une problématique husserlienne de l'inconscient. Husserl et Hegel', in *Edmund Husserl 1859-1959*, The Hague, Nijhoff, 1959, p.221-237.

1960

Fessard, Gaston, s.j., *De l'actualité historique*, 2 vols, Paris, Desclée de Brouwer, 1960, 304pp & 534pp.

Feuerbach, Ludwig, *Manifestes philosophiques, textes choisis, 1839-1845*, tr. Louis Althusser, Paris, Presses Universitaires de France, 1960, 240pp.

Lukács, Georges, *Histoire et conscience de classe. Essai de dialectique marxiste*, tr. K. Axelos & J. Bois, Paris, Editions de Minuit, 1960, collection 'Arguments'.

Maritain, Jacques, *La philosophie morale*, vol. 1, Paris, Gallimard, 1960. Contains section 'L'idéalisme hégélien', p.159-262.

Peperzak, Adrien T. B., *Le jeune Hegel et la vision morale du monde*, The Hague, Nijhoff, 1960, xv-264pp. 2nd edition, 1969.

Recherches internationales, 19, 5-6, 1960. Special number 'Sur le jeune Marx', containing the following relevant articles:
— Bakouradze, O., 'La formation des idées philosophiques de Karl Marx', p.10-35;
— Togliatti, Palmiro, 'De Hegel au marxisme', p.36-52;
— Lapine, Nikolai, 'La première critique approfondie de la philosophie de Hegel par Marx', p.53-71;
— Hoeppner, Joachim, 'A propos de quelques conceptions erronées du passage de Hegel à Marx', p.175-190;
— Gropp, Rugard Otto, 'Système philosophique et histoire de la philosophie chez Hegel et chez Marx', p.207-218.

Touilleux, *abbé* Paul, *Introduction aux systèmes de Marx et de Hegel*, Paris, Desclée de Brouwer, n.d. [1960], vi-184pp.

Brunet, Christian, 'L'ontologie dans l'"Encyklopädie" de Hegel', *Revue de métaphysique et de morale*, 65, 1960, p.449-462.

Dubarle, Dominique, 'Esquisse du problème contemporain de la raison: Hegel', in *La crise de la raison dans la pensée contemporaine*, Paris, Desclée de Brouwer, 1960, p.97-101.

Godelier, Maurice, 'Les structures de la méthode du "Capital" de Karl Marx', *Economie et politique*, 1960, no. 1, p.35-52; no. 2, p.15-36.

Molnar, Erik, 'L'influence de la philosophie de l'histoire de Hegel sur l'historiographie marxiste', *Etudes historiques*, 1, 1960, p.149-162.

Rohrmoser, Günther, 'Schiller et Hegel. La réconciliation esthétique', *Archives de philosophie*, 23, 1960, p.186-206.

Teyssèdre, Bernard, 'Hegel à Stuttgart', *Revue philosophique de la France et de l'étranger*, 1960, no. 2, p.197-227.

Waelhens, Alphonse de, 'Identité et différence: Heidegger et Hegel', *Revue internationale de philosophie*, 14, no. 52, 1960, p.221-237.

1961

Bayer, R., *Histoire de l'esthétique*, Paris, Armand Colin, 1961. Contains section 'Hegel et l'art', p.260-266.

Cottier, Georges Marie-Martin, *Du romantisme au marxisme*, Paris, Alsatia, 1961, 232pp.

Koyré, Alexandre, *Etudes d'histoire de la pensée philsophique*, Paris, Armand Colin, 1961, 329pp. Reprinted by Gallimard, collection 'Idées', 1971.

Cottier, Georges M.M., 'Hegel, la théologie et l'histoire', *Revue thomiste*, janvier-mars 1961, 88-108.

Fessard, Gaston, 'Attitude ambivalente de Hegel en face de l'histoire', *Archives de philosophie*, avril-juin 1961, p.207-241. Also published in *Hegel-Jahrbuch*, Munich, Dobbeck Verlag, 1961, vol. 1, p.25-60.

Findlay, J.N., 'L'actualité de Hegel', *Archives de philosophie*, 24, 1961, no. 3-4, p.480-496.

Gauvin, Joseph, 'Hegeliana. Réflexions sur le congrès de Vienne', *Archives de philosophie*, 24, 1961, no. 2, p.337-340.

Milhau, Jacques, 'Le jeune Marx et ses problèmes', *La Nouvelle critique*, septembre-octobre 1961, p.65-83. Reprinted in his *Chroniques philosophiques*, Paris, Editions Sociales, 1972, p.133-158.

Mouloud, Noel, 'Logique de l'essence et logique de l'entendement chez Hegel', *Revue de métaphysique et de morale*, 66, 1961, p.159-183.

Niel, Henri, 'La suppression de la philosophie à propos de Hegel et de Marx', *Critique*, 174, 1961, p.973-990.

1962

Garaudy, Roger, *Dieu est mort, étude sur Hegel*, Paris, Presses Universitaires de France, 1962, 439pp.

Lévi-Strauss, Claude, *La Pensée sauvage*, Paris, Plon, 1962. Chapter on 'Histoire et dialectique'.

Papaioannou, Kostas, *Hegel. Présentation, choix de textes*, Paris, Seghers, 1962, collection 'Philosophes de tous les temps'.

Serreau, René, *Hegel et l'hégélianisme*, Paris, Presses Universitaires de France, 1962, collection 'Que sais-je?', 128pp. 4th edition 1971.

Sève, Lucien, *La philosophie française contemporaine et sa genèse de 1789 à nos jours*, Paris, Editions Sociales, 1962.

Althusser, Louis, 'Contradiction et sur-détermination: notes pour une recherche', *La Pensée*, 106, 1962, p.3-22. Reprinted in his *Pour Marx* (1965).

Blanchard, Yvon, 'Note sur la philosophie du travail chez Hegel', *Sciences ecclésiastiques*, 14, 1962, p.311-318.

Cottier, Georges M.M., 'Chronique hégélienne', *Revue thomiste*, 4, 1962, p.630-654.

Gardet, Louis, 'Athéisme et marxisme', *Revue thomiste*, 4, 1962, p.655-666.

Grégoire, François, 'L'état hégélien est-il totalitaire? Critique de l'interprétation de J. Maritain', *Revue philosophique de Louvain*, 66, 1962, p.244-253.

Kremer-Marietti, Angèle, 'Hegel et Nietzsche', *Revue des lettres modernes*, 76-77, 1963, p.17-24.

Leclère, H., 'Hegel', in *Catholicisme. Hier-aujourd'hui-demain*, Paris, Letourzey, 1962, vol. 5, colonnes 561-568.

Régnier, Marcel, 'L'association hégélienne internationale', *Archives de philosophie*, 25, 1962, p.606-608.

1963

Chamley, Paul, *Economie politique et philosophie chez Steuart et Hegel*, Paris, Dalloz, 1963, 232pp.

Chevalier, Charles le, *Ethique et idéalisme. Le courant néohégélien en Angleterre. Bernard Bosanquet et ses amis*, Paris, Vrin, 1963, 190pp.

Doubrovsky, Serge, *Corneille et la dialectique du héros*, Paris, 1963.

Garaudy, Roger, *Le Problème hégélien*, Paris, Cahiers du Centre d'Etudes et de Recherches Marxistes, n.d [1963], 32pp.

Henry, Michel, *L'Essence de la manifestation*, 2 vols, Paris, Presses Universitaires de France, 1963, 908pp.

Lacharrière, René de, *Etudes sur la théorie démocratique, Spinoza, Rousseau, Hegel, Marx*, Paris, Payot, 1963. Contains chapter 'Hegel contre la démocratie', p.113-145.

Althusser, Louis, 'Sur la dialectique. De l'inégalité des origines', *La Pensée*, 110, 1963, p.5-46.

Besse, Guy, 'Deux questions sur un article de Louis Althusser', *La Pensée*, 107, janvier-février 1963, p.52-62.

Garaudy, Roger, 'A propos des "Manuscrits de 1844" de Marx et de quelques essais philosophiques', *Cahiers du communisme*, mars 1963, p.107-126.

D'Hondt, Jacques, 'Meurtre dans la cathédrale. La signification de l'art chrétien selon Forster et Hegel', *Revue d'esthétique*, 16, 1963, p.261-289.

Journet, Charles, 'Un affrontement de Hegel et de la sagesse chrétienne', *Nova et vetera*, 38, 1963, p.102-128.

Mouloud, Noël, 'Forme, sens et dialectique dans l'esthétique de Hegel', *Revue esthétique*, 16, 1963, p.33-63.

Mury, Gilbert, 'Matérialisme et hyperempirisme', *La Pensée*, 108, mars-avril 1963, p.38-51.

Queneau, Raymond, 'Premières confrontations avec Hegel', *Critique*, no. 195-6, 1963, p.694-700.

Ritter, Joachim, 'Hegel et la révolution française', *Archives de philosophie*, 26, 1963, p.323-256; p.516-542.

1964

Arvon, Henri, *Feuerbach, sa vie, son œuvre, avec un exposé de sa philosophie*, Paris, Presses Universitaires de France, 1964, 116pp.

Badi, Amir Mehdi, *Hegel et les origines de la pensée contemporaine*, Lausanne, Payot, 1964, 53pp.

Bruaire, Claude, *L'Affirmation de Dieu, essai sur la logique de l'existence*, Paris, Editions du Seuil, 1964.

Bruaire, Claude, *Logique et religion chrétienne dans la philosophie de Hegel*, Paris, Editions du Seuil, 1964, 190pp. Reprinted 1967.

Chapelle, Albert, *Hegel et la religion*, 3 vols, Paris, Editions Universitaires, 1964, 1967 & 1971.

Fleischmann, Eugène, *La Philosophie politique de Hegel*, Paris, Plon, 1964, 402pp. Subtitled 'sous forme de commentaire sur les "Fondements de la philosophie du droit"'.

Fougeyrollas, Pierre, *Contradiction et totalité. Surgissement et déploiements de la dialectique*, Paris, Editions de Minuit, 1964, collection 'Arguments', 251pp.

Sebag, Lucien, *Marxisme et structuralisme*, Paris, Payot, 1964.

Besse, Guy, 'Sur le travail des philosophes communistes', *Cahiers du communisme*, mai 1964, p.138-151.

Bruaire, Claude, 'Idéalisme et philosophie du langage', *Hegel-Jahrbuch*, 1964, p.16-26.

Cornu, Auguste, 'Sur la formation du matérialisme historique', *La Pensée*, 115, mai-juin 1964, p.5-11.

D'Hondt, Jacques, 'Problèmes de la religion esthétique', *Hegel-Jahrbuch*, 1964, p.34-48.

Duméry, Henri, 'Logique et phénoménologie de l'histoire', *Memorias del XIII. congresso internacionale de filosofia*, Mexico, 1964, vol. 6, p.221-231.

Garaudy, Roger, 'Contradiction et totalité dans la Logique de Hegel', *La Revue philosophique de la France et de l'étranger*, 89, 1964, p.67-69.

Goldschmidt, Victor, 'L'abolition de l'esclavage chez Hegel', *Memorias del XIII. congresso internacionale de filosofia*, Mexico, 1964, vol. 6, p.282-290.

Goldschmidt, Victor, 'Etat de nature et pacte de soumission chez Hegel', *Revue philosophique de la France et de l'étranger*, vol. 154, 1964, no. 1, p.45-66.

Hyppolite, Jean, 'Le tragique et le rationnel dans la philosophie de Hegel', *Hegel-Jahrbuch*, 1964, p.9-15.

Prévost, René, 'L'évolution économique vue par Hegel', *Revue d'histoire économique et sociale*, 42, 1964, p.74-88.

Riet, Georges van, 'Y a-t-il un chemin vers la vérité. A propos de l'introduction à la Phénoménologie de l'esprit de Hegel', *Revue philosophique de Louvain*, série 3, 73, 1964, p.466-476.

SECTION FOUR
BOOKS ON HEGEL SINCE 1965

The list includes books and collections of papers relating to Hegel, published in French in Europe since 1965. Articles published separately are not included, because of the sheer volume of them. Scholars wishing to pursue an inventory of articles are referred to Kurt Steinhauer, *Hegel Bibliography*, Munich, New York and Paris, K.G. Saur, 1980, which gives an extensive international listing up to 1975. For the more recent period, the standard FRANCIS or DIALOG databases should be consulted.

1965

Althusser, Louis, *Pour Marx*, Paris, Maspéro, 1965, 263pp.
Rondet, Henri, s.j., *Hégélianisme et christianisme. Introduction théologique à l'étude du système hégélien*, Paris, Lethielleux, 1965, 158pp.
Vancourt, Raymond, *La Pensée religieuse de Hegel*, Paris, Presses Universitaires de France, 136pp. Reprinted 1971.
Wahl, Jean, *L'expérience métaphysique*, Paris, Flammarion, 1965, 240pp.

1966

Chevalier, Jacques, *Histoire de la pensée*, vol. 4, Paris, Flammarion, 1966, 756pp. Subtitled 'La Pensée moderne de Hegel à Bergson'.
Denis, Henri, *Histoire de la pensée économique*, Paris, Presses Universitaires de France, 1966. Section 'La philosophie politique de Hegel', p.372-386.
D'Hondt, Jacques, *Hegel, philosophe de l'histoire vivante*, Paris, Presses Universitaires de France, 1966. 2nd edition 1987.
Droz, Jacques, *Le romantisme allemand et l'état. Résistance et collaboration dans l'Allemagne napoléonienne*, Paris, Payot, 1966, 312pp.
Garaudy, Roger, *La Pensée de Hegel*, Paris, Bordas, 1966, collection 'Pour connaître', 208pp. 2nd edition 1977.
Gadamer, Hans-Georg, editor, *Hegel-Tage Royaumont 1964*, Bonn, Bouvier, 1966. French essays by Marcel Régnier, Jean Hyppolite, Jean Wahl, Joseph Gauvin, André Kaan.
Lacan, Jacques, *Ecrits,* Paris, Editions du Seuil, 1966, collection 'Le champ freudien'.

1967

Derrida, Jacques, *L'Ecriture et la différence*, Paris, Editions du Seuil, 1967. Chapter 9, 'De l'économie restreinte à l'économie générale: un hégélianisme sans réserve'.
D'Hondt, Jacques, *Hegel, sa vie, son œuvre avec un exposé de sa philosophie*, Paris, Presses Universitaires de France, 1967, 119pp. 2nd edition 1975.
George, Waldemar, (pseud. George Jarocinski), *Présence de l'esthétique de Hegel*, Paris, Arted, 1967, 40pp.
Maspétiol, Roland, *Droit, société civile et état dans la pensée de Hegel*, Paris, Sirey, 1967, 37pp.
Soubise, Louis, *Le Marxisme après Marx, 1956-1965: quatre marxistes dissidents français*, Paris, 1967.

Taminiaux, Jacques, *La Nostalgie de la Grèce à l'aube de l'idéalisme allemand*, The Hague, Nijhoff, 1967. Sections 'Le jeune Hegel et l'héllénisme schillerien', p.1-32, 'L'itinéraire de Hegel', p.206-266.

1968

Benz, Ernst, *Les sources mystiques de la philosophie romantique allemande*, Paris, Vrin, 1968, 155pp.

Châtelet, François, *Hegel*, Paris, Editions du Seuil, 1968, 192pp, collection 'Ecrivains de toujours'.

D'Hondt, Jacques, *Hegel en son temps (Berlin 1818-1831)*, Paris, Editions Sociales, 1968, 302pp.

D'Hondt, Jacques, *Hegel secret, recherches sur les sources cachées de la pensée de Hegel*, Paris, Presses Universitaires de France, 1968, collection 'Epiméthée', 348pp. 2nd edition, 'mise à jour', 1986.

Fleischmann, Eugène, *La Science universelle ou la logigue de Hegel*, Paris, Plon, 1968, 387pp.

Garaudy, Roger, *Lénine*, Paris, Presses Universitaires de France, 1968.

Hegel-Jahrbuch 1967, Meisenheim, Hain, 1968. Contains the following French articles:
— Bobbio, Norberto, 'Hegel et l'école de droit naturel', p.9-33;
— Fessard, Gaston, 'Les relations familiales dans la philosophie du droit de Hegel', p.34-63;
— D'Hondt, Jacques, 'L'appréciation de la guerre révolutionnaire par Hegel', p.64-75;
— Bruaire, Claude, 'Abstraction juridique et revendication légitime', p.76-83.

Heidegger, Martin, *Questions*, vol. 2, Paris, Gallimard, 1968. Contains essay 'Hegel et les Grecs'.

Koyré, Alexandre, *Essai d'une histoire raisonnée de la philosophie paienne*, 3 vols, Paris, Gallimard, 1968-1973. Subtitled 'Introduction au Système du Savoir hégélien'.

Labarrière, Pierre-Jean, *Structures et mouvement dialectique dans la Phénoménologie de l'esprit*, Paris, Aubier-Montaigne, 1968, 320pp. Reprinted 1984.

Lacroix, Jean, *Panorama de la philosophie française contemporaine*, Paris, Presses Universitaires de France, 1968.

Palmier, Jean-Michel, *Hegel, essai sur la formation du système hégélien*, Paris, Editions universitaires, 1968, collection 'Classiques du XXe siècle', 125pp.

Rivaud, Albert, *Histoire de la philosophie*, vol. 5, 'De Hegel à Schopenhauer', Paris, Presses Universitaires de France, 1968.

1969

Althusser, Louis, *Lénine et la philosophie*, Paris, Maspero, 1969. Expanded edition printed 1972 under the title *Lénine et la philosophie, suivi de Marx et Lénine devant Hegel*.

L'Arc, Aix-en-Provence, 38, 1969. Special number on Hegel. Includes articles by C. Backès, D. Janicaud, J. D'Hondt, D. Hollier, X. Audouard, M. F. Cassiau, J. Delhomme, H. Wetzel, P. Trotignon, F. Escaraffel.

Bourgeois, Bernard, *La Pensée politique de Hegel*, Paris, Presses Universitaires de France, 1969, 148pp.

La Dialectique. Actes du 14e congrès des sociétés de philosophie de langue française, Paris, Presses Universitaires de France, 1969, 304pp. Includes articles by G. Almaleh, M. Charpy, J. D'Hondt, E. Fleischmann, G. Kirscher, A. Marietti, A. Robinet, R. Araud, D. Dubarle, O. Luttenbacher, G. Fessard, A. Leonard, G. van Riet.

Gadamer, Hans-Georg, ed., *Hegel-Tage Urbino 1965*, Bonn, Bouvier, 1969, 229pp. Includes French articles by Eric Weil, B.-M. Lemaigre, Joseph Gauvin, Jean Hyppolite, Paul Chamley, Claude Bruaire, Marcel Régnier, Gilbert Kirscher, Xavier Tilliette.

Gauthier, Yvon, *L'Arc et le cercle, l'essence du langage chez Hegel et Hölderlin*, Paris & Bruxelles, Desclée de Brouwer, 1969, 229pp.

Heidegger, Martin, *Séminaire du Thor, sur la 'Differenzschrift' de Hegel*, Paris, R. Munier, 1969, 40pp.

Löwith, Karl, *De Hegel à Nietzsche*, tr. Rémi Laureillard, Paris, Gallimard, 1969, 467pp. First published in German in 1941. Reprinted 1981.

Marcuse, Herbert, *Philosophie et Révolution, trois études*, Paris, Denoël-Gonthier, 1969, 156pp.

Ricœur, Paul, *Le conflit des interprétations. Essais d'herméneutique*, Paris, Editions du Seuil, 1969, 512pp.

Sève, Lucien, *Marxisme et théorie de la personnalité*, Paris, Editions Sociales, 1969. 4th edition, 1975.

Vergez, André Michel, *Faute et liberté*, Paris, Les Belles Lettres, 1969, 490pp. Chapter XIII, 'Faute et liberté selon Hegel', p.309-325.

1970

Archives de philosophie, 33, no. 4, 1970. Special number with articles by H.-G. Gadamer, P.-J. Labarrière, O. Poggeler, W. Pannenberg, H. Kimmerle, G. Kirscher, J. Gauvin, J. D'Hondt.

Arvon, Henri, *La philosophie allemande*, Paris, Seghers, 1970, collection 'Philosophies de tous les temps', 222pp.

Boey, le père Conrad, s.j., *L'Aliénation dans la 'Phénoménologie de l'Esprit'*, Paris, Desclée de Brouwer, 1970, 311pp.

Bourgeois, Bernard, *Hegel à Francfort ou judaïsme, christianisme, hégélianisme*, Paris, Vrin, 1970, 125pp.

D'Hondt, Jacques, editor, *Hegel et la pensée moderne*, Paris, Presses Universitaires de France, 1970, 216pp. Papers by Jacques D'Hondt, Jacques Derrida, Louis Althusser, Dominique Dubarle, Dominique Janicaud, Marcel Regnier.

Dialogue, 9, 1970. Special number with articles by Y. Blanchard, K. Hedwig, G. Kortian, O. Reboul, M.E. Williams.

Gouliane, Constantin I., *Hegel ou la philosophie de la crise*, tr. J. Herdan, Paris, Payot, 1970, 443pp.

Hegel-Jahrbuch 1968-69, Meisenheim, Hain, 1970. Contains French essays by 13 contributors.

Hegel, l'esprit objectif, l'unité de l'histoire, Lille, R. Giard, 1970, 348pp. 'Actes du 3e Congrès international pour l'étude de la philosophie de Hegel, Lille, 8-10 avril 1968', some 30 contributions.

Lefebvre, Henri, *La Fin de l'histoire, épilégomènes*, Paris, Editions de Minuit, 1970, 235pp.

Léonard, André, *La Foi chez Hegel,* Paris, Desclée de Brouwer, 1970, 428pp.

Palma, Norman, *Moment et processus, essai de compréhension de la dimension psycho-socio-historico-existentielle de la Logique de l'Encyclopédie de Hegel*, Paris, Ediciones hispanico-americanas, 1970, 363pp.

Revue de métaphysique et de morale, 75, 1970. Special number with articles by M. Conche, G. Hoehn, A. Philonenko, H.-B. Vergote.

Revue de théologie et de philosophie, 20, 1970. Special number with articles by J. D'Hondt, P. Kemp, P. Secretan.

Revue internationale de philosophie, 24, no. 91, 1970. Special number entitled 'Présence de Hegel', with essays by J. D'Hondt, C. I. Gouliane, F. Lombardi, N. Rotenstreich, C. Bruaire, G. Planty-Bonjour.

Ritter, Joachim, *Hegel et la Révolution française*, Paris, Beauchesne, 1970, 144pp.

Rohrmoser, Günther, *Théologie et aliénation dans la pensée du jeune Hegel*, Paris, Beauchesne, 1970, 119pp.

Weil, Eric, *Essais et conférences*, vol. 1, Paris, Plon, 1970.

1971

D'Hondt, Jacques, ed., *Hegel et Marx: la politique et le réel*, Poitiers, Publications de la Faculté des Lettres, 1971. 120pp. A collection of 7 papers by Claude Bruaire, Solange Mercier-Josa, Guy Planty-Bonjour, Claude Orsoni, François Ricci, Pierre Methais, Jacques D'Hondt.

Hommage à Jean Hyppolite, Paris, Presses Universitaires de France, 1971.

Hyppolite, Jean, *Figures de la pensée philosophique, écrits 1931-1968*, 2 vols, Paris, Presses Universitaires de France, 1971, vi-1042pp.

Koyré, Alexandre, *Etudes d'histoire de la pensée philosophique*, Paris, Gallimard, 1971.

1972

Borel, Alain, *Hegel et le problème de la finitude*, Paris, La Pensée Universelle, 1972, 224pp.

Derrida, Jacques, *Marges de la philosophie*, Paris, Editions de Minuit, 1972. Essay 'Le puits et le pyramide. Introduction à la sémiologie de Hegel', p.79-127.

D'Hondt, Jacques, *De Hegel à Marx*, Paris, Presses Universitaires de France, 1972.

Dubarle, Dominique, & André Doz, *Logique et dialectique*, Paris, Larousse, 1972, 246pp.

Gurvitch, Georges, *Dialectique et sociologie*, Paris, 1972.

Lebrun, Gérard, *La Patience du concept, essai sur le discours hégélien*, Paris, Gallimard, 1972, 429pp.

Marcuse, Herbert, *L'Ontologie de Hegel et la théorie de l'historicité*, tr. G. Raulet & H. A. Baatsch, Paris, Editions de Minuit, 1972.

McLellan, David, *Les jeunes hégéliens et Karl Marx*, Paris, Payot, 1972, 237pp.

Milhau, Jacques, *Chroniques philosophiques*, Paris, Editions Sociales, 1972.

Mouloud, Noël, editor, *Les signes et leur interprétation*, Paris, Editions Universitaires, 1972, 191pp. Contains two essays on Hegel.

Quelquejeu, le père Bernard, o.p., *La Volonté dans la philosophie de Hegel*, Paris, Editions du Seuil, 1972, 351pp.

1973

Habermas, Jürgen, *La technique et la science comme idéologie*, Paris, Gallimard, 1973, 221pp. Includes essay 'Travail et interaction. Remarques sur la Philosophie de l'Esprit de Hegel à Iena', p.163-211.

Küng, Hans, *L'Incarnation de Dieu*, Paris, Desclée de Brouwer, 1973, 722pp. Subtitled 'Introduction à la pensée théologique de Hegel comme prolégomènes à une christologie future'.

Litt, Theodor, *Hegel, essai de renouvellement critique*, Paris, Denoël- Gonthier, 1973.

Nancy, Jean-Luc, *La remarque spéculative: un bon mot de Hegel*, Paris, Editions Galilée, 1973, collection 'La Philosophie en effet', 179pp. Subtitled 'Essai sur le concept hégélien d'Aufheben'.

1974

Delbez, Louis. *La Pensée politique allemande*, Paris, R. Pichon & R. Durand-Auzias, 1974, 230pp.

Derrida, Jacques, *Glas*, Paris, 1974.

D'Hondt, Jacques, editor, *Hegel et la pensée grecque*, Paris, Presses Universitaires de France, 1974, 183pp. Essays by Pierre Aubenque, Jeanne Delhomme, Maurice de Gandillac, Dominique Janicaud.

D'Hondt, Jacques, editor, *Hegel et le siècle des lumières*, Paris, Presses Universitaires de France, 1974, 183pp. Essays by Guy Planty-Bonjour, Vitaly Kouznetsov, Marie-Jeanne Königson, Guy Besse, Pierre Methais, Michèle Jalley, Jacques D'Hondt.

Guindey, Guillaume, *Le drame de la pensée dialectique: Hegel, Marx, Sartre*, Paris, Vrin, 1974, 160pp.

Horkheimer, Max, *Les débuts de la philosophie bourgeoise de l'histoire*, tr. Denis Authier, Paris, Payot, 1974, 161pp. Contains essay 'Hegel et le problème de la métaphysique', p.139-158. Reprinted 1980.

Léonard, André-Albert, *Commentaire littéral de la 'Logique' de Hegel*, Paris, Vrin, and Louvain, Editions de l'Institut Supérieur de Philosophie, 1974, 622pp.

Malindey, Henri, *Le legs des choses dans l'œuvre de Francis Ponge*, Lausanne, L'Age d'Homme, 1974, 105pp.

Planty-Bonjour, Guy, *Hegel et la pensée philosophique en Russie. 1830-1917*, The Hague, Nijhoff, 1974, 343pp.

1975

Guibal, Francis, *Dieu selon Hegel. Essai sur la problématique de la Phénoménologie de l'Esprit*, Paris, Aubier-Montaigne, 1975, 352pp.

Janicaud, Dominique, *Hegel et le destin de la Grèce*, Paris, Vrin, 1975, 377pp.

Labica, Georges, *Le Statut marxiste de la philosophie*, Bruxelles, Editions Complexe, 1976, collection 'Dialectiques'.

Lefebvre, Henri, *Hegel, Marx, Nietzsche, ou le Royaume des ombres*, Paris, Casterman, 1975, 224pp.

Lindenberg, Daniel, *Le Marxisme introuvable*, Paris, Calmann-Lévy, 1975, 250pp.

Milhau, Jacques, *Le Marxisme en mouvement*, Paris, Presses Universitaires de France, 1975, 183pp.

1976

Badaloni, Nicola, *Pour le communisme, questions de théorie*, tr. Dominique Grisoni & Robert Maggiori, Paris & The Hague, Mouton, 1976, 264pp.

Brohm, Jean-Marie, *Qu'est-ce que la dialectique?*, Paris, Editions Librairie de la Janquière, 1976, 152pp.

Colletti, Lucio, *Le Marxisme et Hegel*, tr. J.C. Biette & C. Gauchet, Paris, Editions Champ Libre, 1976, 323pp.

Foulquié, Paul, *La Dialectique*, Paris, Presses Universitaires de France, 1976, 127pp.

Khamei, Anvar, *Le Révisionisme de Marx à Mao Tse-toung*, Paris, Anthropos, 1976, 423pp.

Lefebvre, Henri, *De l'Etat*, 3 vols, Paris, Union Générale d'Editions, 1976-77, 381pp, 435pp, 377pp.

Manifestation et révélation, Paris, Beauchesne, 1976, 250pp. Contains in particular a paper by Dominique Dubarle, 'Révélation de Dieu et manifestation de l'Esprit dans la philosophie de la religion de Hegel', p.77-206.

Marx, Karl, *Critique de l'Etat hégélien*, tr. & preface, Kostas Papaioannou, Paris, Union generale d'editions, 1976, 318pp.

Paquet, Marcel, *L'enjeu de la philosophie*, Paris, Editions de la Différence, 1976, 133pp.

1977

Balibar, Etienne et al., *Sur la dialectique*, Paris, Editions Sociales, 1977, 311pp. Essays by Etienne Balibar, Guy Besse, Jean-Pierre Cotten, Pierre Jaeglé, Georges Labica, Jacques Texier.

Bloch, Ernst, *Sujet-Objet. Eclaircissements sur Hegel*, tr. Maurice de Gandillac, Paris, Gallimard, 1977, 498pp.

Cotten, Jean-Pierre, et al., *A propos de Hegel. Sur quelques problèmes actuels*, Paris, Centre d'Etudes et de Recherches Marxistes, 1977, 44pp.

Glucksmann, André, *Les Maîtres penseurs*, Paris, Grasset, 1977, 321pp.

Hegel et la théologie contemporaine: l'absolu dans l'histoire, Neuchâtel, Delachaux & Niestlé, 1977, 256pp.

Juszezak, Joseph, *L'Anthropologie de Hegel à travers la pensée moderne: Marx, Nietzsche, Kojève, Weil*, Paris, Anthropos, 1977, 257pp.

Moinet, Jean-Louis, *Genèse et unification du spectacle*, Paris, Editions Champ Libre, 1977, 316pp.

Muller, Philippe, *Prévision et amour. 1. Le discours nu*, Lausanne, L'Age d'Homme, 1977, 461pp.

1978

Archives de philosophie, 41, 1978. Special number with articles by P.J. Labarrière, Y. Thierry, J. G. Naylor.

Dieng, Amady Aly, *Hegel, Marx, Engels et les problèmes de l'Afrique noire*, Dakar, Sankové, 1978.

D'Hondt, Jacques, *L'Idéologie de la rupture*, Paris, Presses Universitaires de France, 1978, 192pp.

Rihs, Charles, *L'École des jeunes hégéliens et les penseurs socialistes français*, Paris, Anthropos, 1978, 655pp.

Tchang Che-Ying, *Le noyau rationnel de la dialectique hégélienne*, tr. A. Badiou, J. Bellassen, L. Mossot, Paris, Maspero, 1978, 91pp.

Theis, Robert, *Le Discours dédoublé, philosophie et théologie dans la pensée du jeune Hegel*, Paris, Barre-Dayez, 1978, 247pp.

Vieillard-Baron, Jean-Louis, *Le Temps. Platon, Hegel, Heidegger*, Paris, Vrin, 1978, 46pp.

1979

Adorno, Theodor, *Trois études sur Hegel*, Paris, Payot, 1979, 173pp.

Brito, Emilio, s.j., *Hegel et la tâche actuelle de la christologie*, tr. Thierry Dejond, s.j., Paris, Lethielleux, 1979, 394pp.

Hulin, Michel, *Hegel et l'Orient*, Paris, Vrin, 1979, 224pp.

Juszezak, Joseph, *Le procès de la métaphysique: essai d'interprétation de la philosophie post-hégélienne*, Paris, Anthropos, 1979, 284pp.

Labarrière, Pierre-Jean, *La Phénoménologie de l'Esprit de Hegel: introduction à une lecture*, Paris, Aubier-Montaigne, 1979, 287pp.

Macherey, Pierre, *Hegel ou Spinoza*, Paris, Maspero, 1979, 261pp.

Revue de métaphysique et de morale, 84, 1979. Special number with articles by D. Souche-Dagues and P.-J. Labarrière.

Vieillard-Baron, Jean-Louis, *Platon et l'idéalisme allemand 1770-1830*, Paris, Beauchesne, 1979, 408pp.

Weil, Eric, et al., *Hegel et la philosophie du droit*, Paris, Presses Universitaires de France, 1979, 156pp. Contains papers by Eric Weil, Karl-Heinz Ilting, Eugène Fleischmann, Bernard Bourgeois, Jean-Louis Gardies.

1980

Bénoit, Francis-Paul, *Les Idéologies politiques modernes: le temps de Hegel*, Paris, Presses Universitaires de France, 1980, 338pp.

Jarczyk, Gwendoline, *Système et liberté dans la Logique de Hegel*, Paris, Aubier-Montaigne, 1980, 321pp.

Juszczak, Joseph, *Hegel et la liberté*, Paris, Editions CEDES-CDU, 1980, 254pp.

Legros, Robert, *Le Jeune Hegel et la naissance de la pensée romantique*, Paris, Ousia, 1980, 320pp.

Mercier-Josa, Solange, *Lire Marx et Hegel*, Paris, Editions Sociales, 1980, 203pp.

Revue de métaphysique et de morale, 85, 1980. Special number with articles by M. Haar and J.-R. Seba.

Vadée, Michel, editor, *Science et dialectique chez Hegel et Marx*, Paris, Editions du CNRS, 1980, 114pp.

1981

Archives de philosophie, 44, 1981. Special number with articles by P.-J. Labarrière, G. Jarczyk, J.-L. Schlegel, E. Brito, O. Poeggeler.

Biard, Joël, editor, *Introduction à la lecture de la 'Science de la Logique' de Hegel. 1. l'Etre*, Paris, Aubier-Montaigne, 1981, 302pp. Papers by J. Biard, D. Buvat, J.-F. Kervegan, J.-F. Kling, A. Lacroix, A. Lécrivain, M. Slubicki.

Harris, Henry Silton, *Le Développement de Hegel: Vers le soleil 1780-1801*, Lausanne & Paris, L'Age d'Homme, 1981, 511pp.

Longuenesse, Béatrice, *Hegel et la critique de la métaphysique: étude sur la doctrine d'essence*, Paris, Vrin, 1981, 217pp.

Lukács, György, *Le jeune Hegel: sur les rapports de la dialectique et de l'économie*, 2 vols, tr. Guy Haarscher & Robert Legros, Paris, Gallimard, 1981, 446pp & 394pp.

Planty-Bonjour, Guy, ed., *Phénoménologie hégélienne et husserlienne*, Paris, Editions du CNRS, 1981, 133pp. Other contributors include, Paul Ricœur, J. Rolland de Renéville, D. Souche-Dagues, G. Schmidt.

1982

Gérard, Gilbert, *Critique et dialectique. L'Itinéraire de Hegel à Iéna (1801-1805)*, Bruxelles, Facultés Universitaires Saint-Louis, 1982, viii-456pp.

Jacob, André, *Cheminements de la dialectique à l'éthique*, Paris, Anthropos, 1982, 226pp.

Philosophiques, 9, 1982. Special number with articles by L.-P. Luc and P. Gravel.

Planty-Bonjour, Guy, ed., *Hegel et la religion*, Paris, Presses Universitaires de France, 1982, 211pp. Papers by Jacques D'Hondt, Adrien Peperzak, L. Œing-Hanhoff, Karl-Heinz Ilting, Guy Planty-Bonjour, Yirmiahu Yovel, Bernard Bourgeois.

Religion et politique dans les années de formation de Hegel, Lausanne & Paris, L'Age d'Homme, 1982, 164pp. Proceedings of colloquium held at Lausanne, 13-15 November 1981, with papers by L.Hasler, Ch. Jamme, B. Bourgeois, E.E. Harris.

Revue de métaphysique et de morale, 87, 1982. Special number with articles by O. Sozer, D. Souche-Dagues, B. Longuenesse, P. Marignac.

Revue internationale de philosophie, 36, 1982. Special number with articles by B. Bourgeois, J. D'Hondt, K.-H. Ilting, M. Buhr, L. Lugarini, G. Planty-Bonjour.

1983

Biard, Joël, editor, *Introduction à la lecture de la 'Science de la Logique' de Hegel: 2. La doctrine de l'Essence*, Paris, Aubier-Montaigne, 1983, 392pp. Papers by J. Biard, D. Buvat, J.-F. Kervegan, J.-F. Kling, A. Lacroix, A. Lécrivain, M. Slubicki.

Brito, Emilio, *La Christologie de Hegel: 'Verbum Crucis'*, tr. B. Pottier, s.j., Paris, Beauchesne, 1983, 696pp.

Maspétiol, Roland, *Esprit objectif et sociologie hégélienne*, Paris, Vrin, 1983, 124pp.

Opiela, Stanislas, *Le Réel dans la 'Logique' de Hegel: développement et auto-détermination*, Paris, Beauchesne, 1983, 366pp.

Souche-Dagues, Denise, *Logique et politique hégéliennes*, Paris, Vrin, 1983, 133pp.

1984

Borch-Jacobsen, Mikkel, & Michaud, Eric, & Nancy, Jean-Luc, *Hypnoses*, Paris, Editions Galilée, 1984, 149pp.

Denis, Henri, *Logique hégélienne et systèmes économiques*, Paris, Presses Universitaires de France, 1984, 165pp.

D'Hondt, Jacques, *Hegel: le philosophe du débat et du combat*, Paris, Livre de Poche, 1984, 379pp.

Hegel, l'esprit absolu, Ottawa, Editions de l'Universite d'Ottawa, 1984. Proceedings of a colloquium.

Heidegger, Martin, *La 'Phénoménologie de l'Esprit' de Hegel*, tr. Emmanuel Martineau, Paris, Gallimard, 1984, 238pp.

Lefebvre, Jean-Pierre & Macherey, Pierre, *Hegel et la société*, Paris, Presses Universitaires de France, 1984, 128pp.

Marion, Jean-Luce & Planty-Bonjour, Guy, editors, *Phénoménologie et métaphysique*, Paris, Presses Universitaires de France, 1984, 278pp.

Rosenfield, Denis L., *Politique et liberté: une étude sur la structure logique de la 'Philosophie du droit' de Hegel*, Paris, Aubier, 1984, 342pp.

Simon, Hyppolite, *Chrétiens dans l'état moderne ou Comment peut-on être chrétien après Marx et Hegel?*, Paris, Editions du Cerf, 1984, 222pp.

Taminiaux, Jacques, *Naissance de la philosophie hégélienne de l'état: commentaire et traduction de la 'Realphilosophie' de Iéna 1805-6*, Paris, Payot, 1984, 296pp.

1985

Boal, Augusto, *Théâtre de l'opprimé*, tr. Dominique Lemann, Paris, Editions de la Découverte, 1985. Chapter 'Hegel et Brecht: personnage, sujet ou objet', p.153-180.

Bruaire, Claude, *La dialectique*, Paris, Presses Universitaires de France, 1985, 127pp.

Muller, Philippe, *Prévision et amour. 2. Le miroir éclaté,* Lausanne, L'Age d'Homme, 1985, 465pp.

Pöggeler, Otto, *Etudes hégéliennes*, Paris, Vrin, 1985, x-193pp.

Stanguennec, André, *Hegel critique de Kant*, Paris, Presses Universitaires de France, 1985, 356pp.

Vattimo, Gianni, *Les aventures de la différence*, Paris, Editions de Minuit, 1985, 203pp.

1986

Bourgeois, Bernard, *Le Droit naturel de Hegel 1802-03: commentaire*, Paris, Vrin, 1986, 666pp. Subtitled 'Contribution à l'étude de la genèse de la spéculation hégélienne à Iéna'.

Labarrière, Pierre-Jean, & Jarczyck, Gwendoline, *Hegeliana*, Paris, Presses Universitaires de France, 1986, 367pp.

Mercier-Josa, Solange, *Retour sur le jeune Marx*, Paris, Méridiens Klincksieck, 1986, v-195pp. Subtitled 'Deux études sur le rapport de Marx à Hegel dans les Manuscrits de 44 et dans le manuscrit dit de Kreuznach'.

Planty-Bonjour, Guy, editor, *Droit et liberté selon Hegel*, Paris, Presses Universitaires de France, 1986, 264pp.

Souche-Dagues, Denise, *Le Cercle hégélien*, Paris, Presses Universitaires de France, 1986, 187pp.

1987

Biard, Joël, editor, *Introduction à la lecture de la 'Science de la Logique' de Hegel: 3. La doctrine du Concept*, Paris, Aubier-Montaigne, 1987, 548pp. Papers by J. Biard, D. Buvat, J.-F. Kervegan, J.-F. Kling, A. Lacroix, A. Lécrivain, M. Slubicki.

Doz, André, *La Logique de Hegel et les problèmes traditionnels de l'ontologie*, Paris, Vrin, 1987, 325pp.

Harris, Errol Eustace, *Lire la Logique de Hegel: commentaire de la logique de Hegel,* Lausanne, L'Age d'Homme, 1987, 359pp.

Lauth, Reinhardt, *Hegel critique de la doctrine de la science de Fichte*, tr. M. Régnier, s.j., & X. Tilliette, s.j., Paris, Vrin 1987, 186pp.

Papaioannou, Kostas, *Hegel*, Paris, Presses-Pocket, 1987, 253pp.

1988

Harris, Henry Silton, *Le Développement de Hegel: Pensées nocturnes: Iéna 1801-1806,* Lausanne & Paris, L'Age d'Homme, 1988, 543pp.

La Pensée, 262, mars-avril 1988. Special issue entitled 'Que faire avec Hegel?'. Contributors include Lucien Sève, Gwendoline Jarczyk, Pierre-Jean Labarrière, Solange Mercier-Josa, Joël Biard.

Vieillard-Baron, Jean-Louis, & Kaplan, Francis, eds, *Introduction à la philosophie de la religion,* Paris, Editions du Cerf, 1988, 507pp.

Zizek, Slavoj, *Le Plus sublime des hystériques: Hegel passe,* Paris, Point Hors Ligne, 1988, 310pp.

1989

Bras, Gérard, *Hegel et l'art,* Paris, Presses Universitaires de France, 1989, 128pp. Includes selected texts translated by J.P. Lefebvre & J.P. Mathieu.

Pinson, Jean-Claude, *Hegel, le droit et le libéralisme,* Paris, Presses Universitaires de France, 1989, 228pp.

1990

L'Arc, mai 1990, 105pp. Includes articles by C. Backès, D. Janicaud, J. D'Hondt, D. Hollier, X. Audouard, M.-F. Cassiau, J. Delhomme, H. Wetzel, P. Trotignon, F. Escaffarel.

Fessard, Gaston, *Hegel, le christianisme et l'histoire,* Paris, Presses Universitaires de France, 1990, 320pp. Edited and presented by Michel Sales.

Rosenfield, Denis L., *Du mal: essai pour introduire en philosophie le concept du mal,* Paris, Aubier, 1990, 194pp.

Michael Kelly

SECTION FIVE
OTHER WORKS CITED

Simon, Jules, *Victor Cousin*, Paris, Hachette, 1910, 186pp.

Giraud, Victor, *Essai sur Taine*, Paris, Hachette, 1912, 361pp.

Boas, George, *French Philosophers of the Romantic Period*, Baltimore, Johns Hopkins Press, 1925, xi-325pp.

Foucher, Louis, *La Philosophie catholique en France au XIXe siècle avant la renaissance thomiste et dans son rapport avec elle (1800-1880)*, Paris, Vrin, 1955, 280pp.

Charlton, D. G., *Positivist Thought in France during the Second Empire 1852-1870*, Oxford University Press, 1959, 251pp.

Charlton, D. G., *Secular Religions in France 1815-1870*, Oxford University Press, 1963, 250pp.

Evans, Colin, *Taine, essai de biographie intérieure*, Paris, Nizet, 1975, 615pp.

Lukács, Georg, *The Young Hegel*, tr. Rodney Livingstone, London, Merlin, 1975, 576pp.

Poster, Mark, *Existential Marxism in Postwar France*, Princeton University Press, 1975, 416pp.

Kolakowski, Leszek, *Main Currents of Marxism*, tr. P.S. Falla, 3 vols, Oxford University Press, 1978, 434pp, 548pp, & 542pp.

Descombes, Vincent, *Le Même et l'autre*, Paris, Minuit, 1979. Translated as *Modern French Philosophy*, Cambridge University Press, 1980, 192pp.

Steinhauer, Kurt, *Hegel Bibliography: Backgound on the International Reception of Hegel within the Concept of the History of Philosophy*, Munich, New York and Paris, K. G. Saur, 1980, 894pp.

Kelly, Michael, *Modern French Marxism*, Oxford, Blackwell, 1982, 240pp.

Butler, Judith P., *Subjects of Desire. Hegelian Reflections in Twentieth Century France*, New York, Columbia University Press, 1987, 268pp.

Bernard-Paul, Robert, *Antécédents du surréalisme*, University of Ottawa, 1988.

Roth, Michael S., *Knowing and History, Appropriations of Hegel in Twentieth Century France*, Cornell University Press, 1988, 264pp.

Reynolds, Deirdre, 'Mallarmé and Hegel: Speculation and the Poetics of Reflection', *French Cultural Studies*, iv, February 1991, p.71-90 .